Key to map pages

Road map symbols

M74	**Motorway**
16　17	**Motorway junctions** – full, restricted access
Sarn Park Services	**Motorway service area**
- - - - -	**Motorway under construction**
S	**Primary route** – dual, single carriageway, services
	– under construction, narrow
Bala	**Primary destination**
25　26	**Numbered junctions** – full, restricted access
	A road – dual, single carriageway
	– under construction, narrow
	B road – dual, single carriageway
	– under construction, narrow
	Minor road – dual, single carriageway
	Drive or track
2	**Roundabout, multi-level junction**
	Distance in miles
	Tunnel
Toll	**Toll, steep gradient** – points downhill
GLYNDWR'S WAY	**National trail** – England and Wales
SUGAR LOAF	**Railway with station, level crossing, tunnel**
RHEIDOL FALLS	**Preserved railway, level crossing, station, tunnel**
	Tramway
	National boundary
	County or unitary authority boundary
	Car ferry, catamaran
	Passenger ferry, catamaran, hovercraft
(V)　(P)	**Internal ferry** – car, passenger
✈　✈	**Principal airport, other airport or airfield**
THE GOWER	**Area of outstanding natural beauty, National Park, National Forest, Regional park**
	Woodland, Beach – sand, shingle
MONTGOMERY CANAL	**Navigable river or canal**
6　6	**Lock, flight of locks, canal bridge number**
	Caravan or camping sites
🚐 🏠 CF	– CCC* Club Site, Ready Camp Site, Camping in the Forest Site
CS　LS	– CCC Certificated Site, Listed Site
	*Categories defined by the Camping and Caravanning Club of Great Britain
☀ P&R ▲965	**Viewpoint, park and ride, spot height** – in metres
■ ■ ■	**Linear antiquity**

▼ Snowdon Mountain Railway Gail Johnson / Dreamstime

Road map scale

1: 100 000 or 1.58 miles to 1 inch

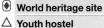

Tourist information

✠ Abbey or priory	🏰 Castle	⚑ Golf course
�🏛 Ancient monument	✝ Cathedral	🏠 Historic house
🐟 Aquarium	🏛 Church of interest	⚓ Historic ship
⊠ Art collection or museum	🏛 Country park	🏯 House and garden
🏛 Art gallery	🐎 County show ground	🏛 Local museum
✕ Battle site and date	🐕 Farm park	**Nature reserve**
🦅 Bird sanctuary	❀ Garden, arboretum	🍁 – National
		RSPB – RSPB
		– Wildlife Trust

⚓ Marina	🐎 Roman antiquity	◉ World heritage site
◈ Maritime or military museum	♈ Safari park	△ Youth hostel
🏁 Motor racing circuit	🛒 Shopping village	🦁 Zoo
🏛 Museum	☺ Sports venue	✦ Other place of interest
Ⓟ Picnic area	🎡 Theme park	
🚂 Preserved railway	ℹ Tourist information centre	
🏃 Racecourse	⬯ Transport collection	

Symbolau Mapiau Heolydd

M74	**Traffordd**
16 — 17	**Cyffordd** – llawn, mynediad cyfyngedig
Sarn Park Services	**Ardal gwasanaethau**
▪▪▪▪▪▪▪	**Yn cael ei hadeiladu**
——S——	**Prif dramwfeydd** – ffordd ddeuol, sengl, gwasanaethau
▪▪▪▪	**– Yn cael ei hadeiladu, ffordd gul**
Bala	**Cyrchfannau'r prif dramwyfeydd**
25 — 26	**Cyffordd** – llawn, mynediad cyfyngedig
———	**Ffordd A** – ffordd ddeuol, sengl
▪▪▪	**– Yn cael ei hadeiladu, ffordd gul**
———	**Ffordd B** – ffordd ddeuol, sengl
▪▪▪	**– Yn cael ei hadeiladu, ffordd gul**
———	**Ffordd arall**
▪▪▪▪▪	**Lon neu rhodfa**
⊕ 2	**Cylchfan, cyffordd ar fwy nag un lefel**
	Peiliter – mewn millitiroedd
)——(	**Twnnel**
Toll ←	**Toll, graddiant serth** – mae'r saeth yn anelu lawr y rhiw
🚶 GLYNDWR'S WAY	**Llwybrau cenedlaethol**
SUGAR LOAF ╫ ─ ─ ─(	**Rheilffordd gyda gorsaf, croesfan wastad, twnnel**
RHEIDOL FALLS ╫ ─ ─ ─(	**Rheilffordd wedi'u ddiogelu gyda croesfan wastad, gorsaf, twnnel**
	Tramffordd
▪▪▪▪▪	**Ffin cenedilaethol**
▪▪▪▪▪	**Ffin sir, awdurdod unedol**
⛴ ⛴	**Fferi cerbydau, catamarán**
⛴ ⛴ ⛴	**Fferi teithwyr, catamarán, hofranlong**
─(V)─ ─(P)─	**Fferi mewnol** – cerbydau, teithwyr
✈ ⊕	**Prif maes awyr, maes awyr arall**
THE GOWER	**Ardal o harddwch nauriol eithrialadol, parc cenedlaethol, parc coedwig**
	Coedtir, Traeth – tywod, graean bas
MONTGOMERY CANAL	**Afon neu gamlas tramwy**
─(6 ⊏⊐ 6)─	**Loc, rhes o lociau, rhif bont camlas**
	Meysydd carafanau neu wersylla
🚐 🏠 CF	**– Safle Clwb CCC*, Maes Gwersylla Parod, Gwersylla yn y Safle Coedwig**
CS LS	**– Safle Tystysgrif CCC, Safle Rhestredig**
	*Categoriau a ddiffinnir gan Glwb Gwersylla a Charafanio Prydain Fawr (CCC)
☼ P&R ▲965	**Gwylfa, park and ride, spot uchder** – mewn medrau
▪▪▪▪▪	**Hynafiaeth llinol**

Graddfa mapiau heol

1: 100 000 • 1 modfedd = 1.58 milltiroedd

0   1   2   3   4   5 km

0   1   2   3 miles

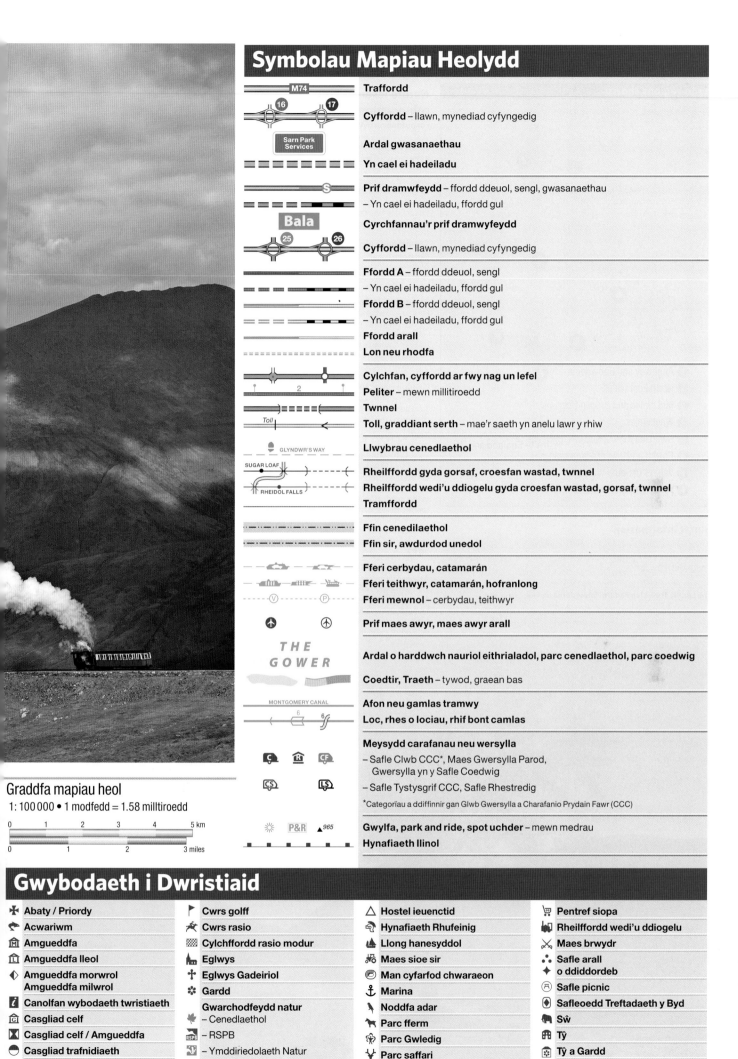

Gwybodaeth i Dwristiaid

⚓ **Abaty / Priordy**	⚑ **Cwrs golff**	△ **Hostel ieuenctid**	🛒 **Pentref siopa**
Acwariwm	**Cwrs rasio**	**Hynafiaeth Rhufeinig**	**Rheilffordd wedi'u ddiogelu**
🏛 **Amgueddfa**	🏁 **Cylchfford rasio modur**	**Llong hanesyddol**	✕ **Maes brwydr**
🏛 **Amgueddfa lleol**	**Eglwys**	**Maes sioe sir**	**Safle arall**
◆ **Amgueddfa morwrol Amgueddfa milwrol**	✝ **Eglwys Gadeiriol**	◎ **Man cyfarfod chwaraeon**	✚ **o ddiddordeb**
ℹ **Canolfan wybodaeth twristiaeth**	❋ **Gardd**	⚓ **Marina**	Ⓟ **Safle picnic**
🏰 **Casgliad celf**	**Gwarchodfeydd natur**	**Noddfa adar**	🏛 **Safleoedd Treftadaeth y Byd**
✕ **Casgliad celf / Amgueddfa**	– **Cenedlaethol**	**Parc fferm**	🐾 **Sŵ**
● **Casgliad trafnidiaeth**	RSPB – **RSPB**	**Parc Gwledig**	🏠 **Tŷ**
🏯 **Castell**	– **Ymddiriedolaeth Natur**	**Parc saffari**	🏠 **Tŷ a Gardd**
	🏛 **Henebion**	🎡 **Parc thema**	

Visitor information

Key to regions shown

1. Anglesey and Snowdonia
2. North East Wales
3. Mid Wales and Brecon Beacons
4. West Wales
5. Swansea, Gower and Vale of Neath
6. Cardiff and Vale of Glamorgan
7. Valleys of South Wales
8. Wye Valley and Vale of Usk

Tourist information

Many Welsh attractions are closed in winter; call to check if a venue is open out of season before making a special trip. Good all-round information is provided by www.visitwales.com.

▼ **The Lonely Tree, Llyn Padarn, Snowdonia** Paul Shields / Dreamstime

Outdoors

Nature reserves and conservation areas

For outdoor activities, see Sports

Anglesey and Snowdonia

RSPB Conwy Nature Reserve
Llandudno Junction / Cyffordd Llandudno, Conwy A feeding and roosting site for ducks, geese and wading birds, with short nature trails, a Visitor Centre, binocular hire and hides. 🖥www.rspb.org.uk **69 D6**

Cardiff and Vale of Glamorgan

Flat Holm Island *Barry / Y Barri, Vale of Glamorgan* A nature reserve accessed by summer boat trips from Barry harbour. **4 C4**

Glamorgan Heritage Coast
Porthcawl, Bridgend A beautiful c.25km stretch of protected coastline with great ecological diversity on its rocky and sandy beaches, coves, dunes and cliffs. There is a Visitor Centre (Dunraven Park, Southerndown) with an information point, the Seawatch Centre maritime interpretation centre in a former coastguard station at Summer-house Point, and the Glamorgan Heritage Coast walk. **2 B4**

Kenfig National Nature Reserve
Ton Kenfig, Pyle / Y Pîl, Bridgend An important conservation site and Site of Special Scientific Interest on the site of a once-thriving town that was engulfed by sand, now home to thousands of animals and plant species, including the rare fen orchid. There is an Information Centre with interactive displays for children. 🖥www.northwaleswildlifetrust.org.uk **10 F2**

Parc Slip Reserve *Tondu, Bridgend* A reserve on the site of an old colliery and open-cast coal workings, with grassland, wildflower meadows, wetlands and woodlands providing habitats for diverse wildlife and a network of footpaths. **10 F4**

Mid Wales and Brecon Beacons

Glaslyn *near Staylittle, Powys* A 540-acre Montgomeryshire Wildlife Trust reserve, including the best area of heather moorland within the Plynlimon Site of Special Scientific Interest and four other habitat types, plus a scenic lake that sometimes attracts diving ducks and wintering Greenland white-fronted geese. Moorland birds include skylarks and ring ouzels, and red kites and other birds of prey are often seen. 🖥www.montwt.co.uk **45 E7**

Lake Vyrnwy *Brynawel, Llanwddyn, Powys* A 16,000-acre RSPB reserve based around an artificial lake: the 90 species of breeding birds include goosanders, common sandpipers and great crested grebes. Information centre and shop. See also Lake Vyrnwy Sculpture Trail (see *Art and crafts*). 🖥www.rspb.org.uk **54 E5**

Llyn Coed Y Dinas *Welshpool / Y Trallwng, Powys* A 20-acre wetland reserve, more than half of which is taken up by a lake filling a gravel pit from which material was taken for construction of a nearby bypass, attracting sand martins (for which there is an information hide), little-ringed plover and roosting wildfowl, including Arctic whooper swans. There is a circular wheelchair-friendly path. 🖥www.montwt.co.uk **47 B8**

Severn Farm Pond *Welshpool / Y Trallwng, Powys* A 3-acre urban educational reserve providing a 'countryside oasis' in a built-up area, centred around a pond with a reed swamp attracting reed buntings. There is a wheelchair-accessible hide for observing birdlife, which includes moorhens, mallards, coots, mute swans and ruddy ducks, and a scented meadow area for visually impaired visitors. 🖥www.montwt.co.uk **47 B8**

Swansea, Gower and Vale of Neath

Bishop's Wood Reserve *Caswell, Swansea* A nature reserve above Caswell Bay, with a countryside centre, guided tours by appointment and year-round activities and events. **9 E6**

Pant-y-Sais Fen *Port Talbot, Neath Port Talbot* A nature reserve and Site of Special Scientific Interest (it is one of the few remaining wetlands in the area), with walks along boardwalks through the fen area and along the towpath of the neighbouring Tennant Canal. **9 D9**

Valleys of South Wales

Taf Fechan Nature Reserve *Merthyr Tydfil / Merthyr Tudful, Merthyr Tydfil* A 102-acre Site of Special Scientific Interest attracting birds such as tawny owls and great-spotted woodpeckers and containing an old tramway that

led to Cyfarthfa Ironworks (which retains late 18th-century blast furnac and calcining kilns), plus the ruins of disused fulling and corn mills. There is a picnic site at the north end by the historic Pontsarn Viaduct, at the bord with Brecon Beacons National Park (se *National Parks and AONBs*). 🖥www. welshwildlife.org/nature-reserves **25 F5**

West Wales

Cardigan Bay Special Area of Conservation *Aberarth, Ceredigion* An internationally important marine wildlife area with some 130 protected bottlenose dolphins and a variety of marine animals and plants living on the rocky reef of the Sarnau at Walloc 🖥www.cardiganbaysac.co.uk **38 F2**

Ceredigion Heritage and Marine Heritage Coast *New Quay / Ceinewydd, Ceredigion* A marine wildlife habitat extending over about a third of Ceredigion's spectacular coastline, with a coastal footpath between Borth (see *Beaches and Resorts*) and Aberystwyth (see *Towns and Villages*) via Clarach. In summer guided walks, talks and boat trips take place along the coastline. 🖥www.ceredigion.gov.uk **31 A7**

Cors Goch Glan Teifi / Cors Caron *Tregaron, Ceredigion* One of Europe's largest growing peat bogs, providing a home for dozens of rare plant and animal species, including the red kite and more than 170 bird species, amor them hen harriers and sparrowhawks The Old Railway Walk is accessible at all times but a permit is needed for the rest of the site. 🖥https:// naturalresources.wales **39 F6**

Gwarchodfa Natur Cenedlaethol Dyfi National Nature Reserve *Ynyslas, Borth / Y Borth, Ceredigion* A nature reserve with a sandy beach and spectacular dunes at the mouth of the River Dyfi. There is a Visitor Centre, a network of footpaths . 🖥https:// naturalresources.wales **44 E3**

Ramsey Island RSPB Reserve *St David's / Tyddewi, Pembrokeshire* An island where you can see migrating birds (Britain's first indigo bunting was spotted here), with colonies of guillemots, razorbills, kittiwakes and more. 🖥www.rspb.org.uk **18 E2**

RSPB Ynys-Hir Reserve *Eglwysfach, Ceredigion* A reserve on the south side of the Dyfi estuary, attracting almost 70 species of breeding birds, including pied flycatchers, treecreepers and woodpeckers. There is a Visitor Centre guided walks, the most extensive network of trails in Wales, and bird-watching hides. 🖥www.rspb.org.uk **44 D4**

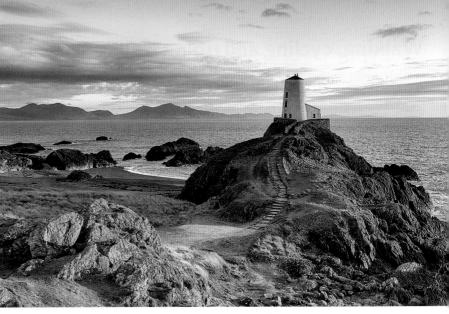

...omer, Skokholm and Grassholm
...arloes, Pembrokeshire Three islands ...here you can see colonies of puffins, ...uillemots, razorbills and many other ...rds close up, as well as grey seals ...d passing porpoises and dolphins. ...omer, a National Nature Reserve, ...s the world's biggest colony of Manx ...earwaters; activity in the nesting ...urrows is relayed to video screens in ...e barn. Grassholm, an RSPB reserve, ...s the north Atlantic's second largest ...olony of gannets.
www.welshwildlife.org **16 C1**

...estfield Pill Neyland, ...embrokeshire A Wildlife Trust reserve ...a dammed pill where waterbirds ...ch as little grebes, ducks, waders ...d kingfishers can be seen, as well as ...oodland birds. The Brunel Trail runs ...ongside (see Outdoors: Walking, ...ding and cycling trails).
www.welshwildlife.org **17 C5**

...ational Parks and ...ONBs

...nglesey and Snowdonia

...nglesey AONB Isle of Anglesey ...n AONB taking in almost the entire ...nglesey coastline, from steep ...nestone cliffs and sandy beaches in the ...ast to rolling sand dunes in the south ...est. ☐www.anglesey.gov.uk **66 B3**

...nowdonia National Park/Parc ...enedlaethol Eryri Gwynedd ...he second largest National Park in ...e country, covering most of the ...ounty of Gwynedd and containing ...e Snowdonia mountain ranges and ...ambrian Coast.
...https://snowdonia.gov.wales **59 D8**

...id Wales and Brecon Beacons

...recon Beacons National Park/ Parc ...enedlaethol Bannau Brycheiniog ...banus, Powys A 1,344sq km National ...ark with stunning mountains and ...oorland; activities include walking, ...cling, riding, sailing, canoeing, ...shing, caving and rock climbing, and ...ere are nature reserves, ancient cave ...stems, the 100ft Henryhyd waterfall, ...ne of Britain's highest), Llangors Lake ...ith Wales's only known crannog, or ...efensive island) and relics of industrial ...eritage. There is a Visitor Centre at ...banus ☐www.breconbeacons.org
...4 B4
...arks and gardens Glanusk Park and ...state Towns and villages Brecon ...eligious buildings Llanthony ...riory Transport Brecon and ...lonmouthshire Canal • Brecon ...lountain Railway Activity centres ...angorse Multi Activity Centre ...iding Cantref Riding Centre

...wansea, Gower and ...ale of Neath

...ower Peninsula Rhossili, Swansea ...ritain's first designated AONB, with a ...astline of spectacular cliffs, isolated ...oves, golden beaches and tidal ...lands. One of the most picturesque ...oots is Three Cliffs Bay, accessed via a ...eep path. Much of the land is owned

by Rhossili National Trust, which has a Visitor Centre at the Coastguard Cottages in Rhossili, with exhibitions. ☐www.explore-gower.co.uk **8 E3**
Beaches and resorts Caswell Bay, Langland Bay, Llangennith, The Mumbles, Port Eynon and Horton, Rhossili, Tor Bay *Castles* Weobley Castle *Houses and gardens* Oxwich Castle *Local history* Gower Heritage Centre *Riding* Pembrey Park Riding Centre *Watersports* Welsh Surfing Federation Surf School

Various regions

Cambrian Mountains Rhayader / Rhaeadr Gwy, Carmarthenshire, Ceredigion and Powys An area proposed as a National Park in 1972 but never officially designated as such, encompassing Plynlimon, the highest mountain in mid Wales, wooded valleys and gorges, rolling moorlands, and the huge upland area of Elenydd, much of which is a Site of Special Scientific Interest. **33 B8**
Factories, mills and mines Felin Newydd Watermill

West Wales

Pembrokeshire Coast National Park Newport / Trefdraeth, Pembrokeshire Britain's only coastal national park, with a strenuous 300km (10- to 15-day) coast path around spectacular bays and headlands, including Cemaes Head, Dinas Island, Carregwastad Point, Strumble Head (see *Other natural features*) and St David's Peninsula. Walkers' buses are provided at various points. There are guided walks and year-round activities and events, including puppet shows, boat trips, pony trekking and canoeing. Haroldston Chins near Broad Haven has an award-winning wheelchair-accessible clifftop viewing point. ☐www.pembrokeshirecoast.wales **19 B8**

Wye Valley and Vale of Usk

Wye Valley (Dyffryn Gwy) Monmouth / Trefynwy, Monmouthshire An AONB straddling the border between England and Wales; the Lower Wye Gorge between Chepstow and Symonds Yat is characterised by spectacular limestone cliffs and a narrow floodplain. Outdoor pursuits include walking (including the long-distance Wye Valley Walk and Offa's Dyke Path; see *Walking, riding and cycling trails*), fishing, canal-cruising, golf, cycling, canoeing and gliding. **27 E8**
Towns and villages Chepstow
Religious buildings Tintern Abbey

Country, coastal and forest parks

Anglesey and Snowdonia

Great Orme Country Park Llandudno, Conwy A limestone headland designated a Special Area of Conservation, Site of Special Scientific Interest and Heritage Coast, containing some famous Kashmiri goats and the Great Orme Bronze Age Copper Mines. The Visitor Centre has interactive displays and a live camera link to a seabird colony. ☐www.conwy.gov.uk **68 C5**

Gwydyr Forest Park Betws-y-Coed, Conwy A forest park ranging across eastern Snowdonia's hills, with more than 20 miles of trails through mountain forest, plus riding, canoeing and mountain biking. **60 C3**

Holyhead Breakwater Country Park Holyhead / Caergybi, Isle of Anglesey A disused quarry with a large seabird population, nature trails and a Visitor Centre. **66 C1**

Padarn Country Park Llanberis, Gwynedd Nature, woodland and industrial trails, the Welsh Slate Museum, craft workshops, a water-sports centre, the Llanberis Lake Railway, Lon Las Peris – family cycling track and an adventure playground. ☐https://snowdonia.gov.wales **59 B7**

Cardiff and Vale of Glamorgan

Bedford Park Cefn Cribwr, Bridgend A 40-acre site comprising ancient woodlands and meadows full of wildflowers and fauna, waymarked nature trails (the main 1.5km footpath and cycle route follows part of the old industrial Dyffryn, Llynvi and Porthcawl railway), picnic sites, play areas and the ruins of industrial buildings. **10 F4**
Factories, mills and mines Cefn Cribwr Ironworks

Bryngarw Country Park Brynmenyn, Bridgend A 113-acre site with woodlands, wetlands, formal gardens (including a Japanese Garden with magnolia, cherry trees and maples, and a Tea Garden pavilion), open pastures, waymarked nature trails, and an ornamental lake, plus an adventure playground, picnic spots and a Visitor Centre. **11 E5**

Cosmeston Lakes Country Park Lavernock Rd, Penarth, Vale of Glamorgan An attractive 200-acre site embracing woodlands, meadows, lakes, a Site of Special Scientific Interest with rare plant and animal species, nature trails, an adventure playground, picnic areas and Visitor Centre. ☐www.valeofglamorgan.gov.uk

4 C3 *Local history* Cosmeston Medieval Village

Porthkerry Country Park Barry / Y Barri, Vale of Glamorgan A 220-acre area of parkland with woods, meadows, nature trails leading to the seashore, mini-golf and a picnic and barbecue area. ☐www.valeofglamorgan.gov.uk **4 C1**

Mid Wales and Brecon Beacons

Craig y Nos Country Park Brecon Rd, Pen-y-cae, Powys A 40-acre country park run by the Brecon Beacons National Park (see *National Parks and AONBs*), set in the historic gardens of Craig y Nos Castle, built by opera singer Dame Adelina Patti. There is a restored Victorian pavilion, a hay meadow, walking trails and a Visitor Centre. **24 D1**

North East Wales

Greenfield Valley Heritage and Country Park Holywell / Treffynon, Flintshire A park containing St Winefride's Well (see *Religious buildings*), the ruins of the 12th-century Basingwerk Abbey and various mill buildings (many of them scheduled ancient monuments), a reconstructed Victorian school, farmhouses, five lakes and woodland walks. There is also a farm museum and a museum about naturalist and explorer Thomas Pennant. ☐www.greenfieldvalley.com **71 D5**

Loggerheads Country Park Denbighshire Woodland trails and guided walks including an Industrial Trail tracing the history of lead mining in the park. The focus of the park is the Tea Gardens by the river Alyn. There are restored mill buildings and an AONB Information Centre. **62 B4**

Moel Famau Country Park Ruthin / Rhuthun, Denbighshire One of Wales's biggest country parks, covering about 2000 acres of uplands and containing the remains of three hillforts dating from 500BC to 43AD and an 11km stretch of the Offa's Dyke Trail, and providing a home to many bird of prey species. **62 B4**

Ty Mawr Country Park Cae Gwilym Lane, Cefn-mawr, Wrexham A wildlife-rich, organically farmed country park on the banks of the Dee, with hay meadows, animal feeding sessions, a play area, a Visitor Centre and panoramic views. **63 F6**

Swansea, Gower and Vale of Neath

Afan Forest Park Afan Argoed, Cynonville, Neath Port Talbot A park containing one of south Wales's loveliest valleys, with a Visitor Centre

hosting exhibitions on its history, wildlife and woodlands, facilities for walking, cycling, orienteering, pony-trekking and picnics, Glyncorrwg Ponds (three fishing lakes, plus canoeing and rowing), and Roman, Iron Age and Bronze Age remains and cairns. **10 C3**
Local history
South Wales Miners Museum

Clyne Valley Country Park Gowerton / Tre-Gwyr, Swansea A large, peaceful country park with a gentle 8km footpath and cycletrack to Gowerton, continuing along the Celtic Trail (see *Walking, riding and cycling trails*) into Carmarthenshire and Pembrokeshire. **9 D7**

Craig Gwladys Cilfrew, Neath Port Talbot A park on a wooded hillside, with way marked forest footpaths, waterfalls, brooks, the remains of old levels, driftmines and tram roads, picnic sites and superb views of the Lower Neath Valley. **10 B2**

Glantawe Riverside Park Pontardawe, Neath Port Talbot An informal countryside recreation area on the site of a reclaimed tinplate works, with footpaths linking to the Swansea canal towpath and a cycleway network connecting with the Cwmtawe Cycleway (see *Walking, riding and cycling trails*). **10 B1**

Gnoll Country Park Neath / Castell-nedd, Neath Port Talbot A country park based on an 18th-century landscaped garden, with lakes, waterfalls, a grotto, a play area and adventure playground, a Visitor Interpretation Centre, and forest footpaths linking to the Mosshouse Reservoir and Cefn Morfudd historical viewpoints. ☐www.neath-porttalbot.gov.uk **10 E3**

Margam Country Park Margam, Neath Port Talbot An 850-acre parkland with historic gardens, walking trails, a Tudor-Gothic style Victorian mansion, an 18th-century orangery, a Victorian vine-house, a 12th-century chapterhouse, a narrow-gauge railway, a bird of prey rescue centre, a farm trail, a pets' corner, deer, an adventure playground, a 'Fairytale Village' and a Visitor Centre. **10 E3**

Valleys of South Wales

Parc Bryn Bach Merthyr Rd, Tredegar, Blaenau Gwent A 40-acre area of wood-lands and pastures on a former industrial site, with a watersports lake, hang-gliding, walking trails and orienteering, an adventure playground, play and picnic areas, and a Countryside Centre with an interpretation unit, lakeside café and bunkhouse accommodation. **25 E7**

Walking, cycling and riding trails

▲ Mountain biking in Afan Forest Park Victor Lucas / Dreamstime

See also: Pembrokeshire Coast National Park (*National Parks and AONBs*), Glamorgan Heritage Coast (*Nature reserves and conservation areas*), Preseli Hills (*Other natural features*)

For more information on these and other trails, visit the Ramblers' Association's website (www.ramblers.org.uk) or the nearest tourist information office.

For more information on the National Cycle Network, see www.sustrans.org.uk.

For mountain-biking and pony-trekking, see *Sports*.

Anglesey and Snowdonia

Lôn Las Cymru (Welsh National Cycle Route) *Holyhead/Caergybi, Isle of Anglesey* A c.350km route forming part of the developing National Cycle Network, taking in minor road and cycle paths and passing through Brecon Beacons/Bannau Brycheiniog and Snowdonia/Eryri National Parks (see *National Parks and AONBs*). **66 C2**

Marin Trails *Betws-y-Coed, Conwy* Marked mountain biking trails from the centre of Betws-y-Coed, linking challenging climbs and fire-road descents winding past waterfalls, lakes, mountain vistas and river valleys in the Gwydyr forest. **60 C3**

Cardiff and Vale of Glamorgan

Taff Trail *Cardiff/Caerdydd, Cardiff* A long-distance walking and cycle trail passing through the often spectacular scenery of the Taff Valley on the old Brecon and Merthyr railway line from Cardiff to Brecon. **4 A3**

Valeways Millennium Heritage Trail *St Fagans/Sain Fagan, Cardiff* A 100km walk through spectacular scenery, divided into 16 routes and taking in the remnants of industrial heritage dating back 6,000 years. **4 A2**

Mid Wales and Brecon Beacons

Glyndwr's Way *from Knighton to the Montgomery Canal, Welshpool/Y Trallwng, Powys* A c.200km walking trail dedicated to 15-century warrior Owain Glyndwr, taking in open moorland, rolling farmland, woodland and forests. **47 B8**

Radnor Ring (Regional Route 25) *Llandrindod Wells/Llandrindod, Powys* A dramatic c.110km circular waymarked ride through rural mid Wales, part of the National Cycle Network, with off-road alternatives for mountain bikers. **41 F6**

North East Wales

Clywedog Trail *Wrexham/Wrecsam, Wrexham* A nine-mile trail exploring the industrial heritage of Wrexham, starting at Minera Lead Mines (see *Factories, mills and mines*) and taking in Nant Mill, Bersham Ironworks and Heritage Centre and the Erddig estate on its way to the town of Wrexham. **63 D7**

North Wales Path *Prestatyn, Denbighshire* A path following the coast and lower mountain slopes between Prestatyn and Bangor. **70 C3**

Offa's Dyke Path *Prestatyn, Denbighshire* A 176-mile path from Prestatyn to Sedbury Cliffs near Chepstow, roughly following the line of an ancient dyke built by Offa, King of Mercia, about 1200 years ago and offering a wide variety of countryside. **70 C3**

Swansea, Gower and Vale of Neath

Coed Morgannwg Way *Margam, Neath Port Talbot* A c.50km route across Morgannwg Forest and Afan Forest Park (see *Country, Coastal and Forest Parks*), following Celtic trackways and passing several Bronze and Iron Age Settlements. **10 E2**

Cwmtawe Cycleway *Pontardawe, Neath Port Talbot* A cycleway along the River Tawe – National Cycle Network route 43. **10 B1**

Swansea Bay Foreshore Path *Black Pill, Swansea* A mostly flat walking and cycling route from Mumbles to Swansea Marina. **9 D7**

Various regions

Celtic Trail (Lôn Geltaidd) *Fishguard/Abergwaun, Monmouthshire to Pembrokeshire* A continuous multi-stage signposted cycle route, via the Gwaun Valley, Tenby, Pembroke Dock, and St David's, taking in Brecon Beacons and Pembrokeshire Coast National Parks (see *National Parks and AONBs*) and forming part of the developing National Cycle Network. **19 B7**

West Wales

Bluestones Cycle Routes *Moylgrove, Pembrokeshire* Ten rides (six road, four mountain, varying from about 20km to 40km) covering the area from Ceibwr Bay and Moylgrove in the north to Llys Y Fran and Llanycefn in the south, and from Llanychaer and Puncheston in the west to Crymych in the east. **30 D2**

Brunel Trail *from Brunel Quay, Neyland, Pembrokeshire* A well-signposted c.20km cycle route along quiet lanes, bridleways and part of the former Great Western Railway, built by Isambard Kingdom Brunel. **17 D5**

Canaston Cycle Trails *Canaston Bridge, Pembrokeshire* Purpose-built signed mountain biking trails through woodland, from easy family tracks to unsurfaced muddy bridleways. **17 B7**

Dylan Thomas Ceredigion Trail *from Llanon to Llangrannog, via Talsarn, Aberaeron, Ceredigion* A three-day walking trail opened in 2003 (the 50th anniversary of the writer's death) to celebrate the places he visited and venues where he lived, stayed and drank, many of which are associated with his most famous work, 'Under Milk Wood'. **38 F2**

Landsker Borderlands *Whitland/Hendy-Gwyn, Carmarthenshire* A c.100km walking trail straddling the historic Landsker Line. **20 D3**

Landsker Cycle Ways *Narberth/Arberth, Pembrokeshire* A network of about 200 signed road routes split into 13 rides of between 5km and 35km. **20 E2**

Last Invasion Trail *Goodwick/Wdig, Pembrokeshire* A c.20km hilly cycle route visiting the sites of the 1797 invasion of Britain by the French, who landed at Carregwastad Point (at a spot marked by a stone monument) and surrendered on Goodwick Sands. **19 B6**

Miner's Way Trail *around Saundersfoot, Kilgetty, Pembrokeshire* A short circular route taking in sites relating to local industrial heritage. **17 C8**

Withybush Woods *Haverfordwest/Hwlffordd, Pembrokeshire* A gentle 1.5km trail suitable for physically and visually handicapped people, with an audio trail. **16 A4**

Wye Valley and Vale of Usk

Sirhowy Valley Walk *Newport/Casnewydd, City and County of Newport* A challenging c.40km ridgeway walk. **13 E6**

Usk Valley Walk *Caerleon/Caerllion, City and County of Newport* An 80km waymarked walk through the river valley. **13 D6**

Parc Cwm Darran *Deri, Bargoed/Bargod, Caerphilly* A tranquil country park in the Darran Valley, with wildflower meadows, woodlands, lakeside paths, scenic trails and cycle paths, and containing the Cwmllwydrew Meadows nature reserve and the restored remains of the powder-store of Olgivie Colliery (one of the last surviving in Wales). www.breconbeacons.org **12 B2**

Parc Penallta *Ystrad Mynach, Caerphilly* A new country park on a former coal tip, with an observatory with spectacular views, a large earth sculpture of a pit pony, woodland, grasslands and a wetland area with a boardwalk, and access to Route 47 of the National Cycle Network leading to the Sirhowy Valley. **12 C2**

Pen-y-fan Pond Country Park *near Croespenmaen, Caerphilly* A popular summer family destination based around one of Wales's last remaining canal-feeder reservoirs, with flat open parkland for rambling, kite-flying and picnicking. It is the starting point for countryside walks around Manmoel. **12 B3**

West Wales

Canolfan Bwlch Nant Yr Arian Forest Centre *Llywernog, Ponterwyd, Ceredigion* A forest centre with panoramic views down the Melindwr Valley to Cardigan Bay and through the forest to Llywernog Uchaf lake. There is live footage of nesting rare red kites and other birds of prey, including kestrels and buzzards, walking and orienteering trails, and a mountain-bike zone. **39 B7**

Gelli Aur Country Park *Dryslwyn, Carmarthenshire* A 60-acre wooded park surrounding an impressive mansion, with nature trails, guided tours, a deer park, an arboretum, terrace gardens, a Visitor Centre with exhibitions and craft demonstrations, and a play area. www.carmarthenshire.gov.uk **22 C4**

Llyn Llech Owain Country Park *Gorslas, near Cross Hands, Carmarthenshire* A 26-acre park with woodland, lakeside and peat bog walks, a mountain-bike trail, a ranger service, an adventure playground and a Visitor Centre with live footage of nesting birds. www.carmarthenshire.gov **22 E4**

Llys-y-Fran Country Park *Llys-y-Fran, Pembrokeshire* A country park focused around a dam and reservoir circled by an 11km foot- and cycle-path, plus picnic sites, a Visitor Centre and exhibition, and surrounding woodland with wildflowers and birdlife. Water sports include paddle boarding, kayaking, canoeing and open water swimming. Equipment can be hired. www.pembrokeshire.gov.uk **19 E8**

Millennium Coastal Park *North Dock, Llanelli, Carmarthenshire* A 20km stretch of coastline on the Burry Estuary, overlooking the dramatic Gower Peninsula (see *National Parks and AONBs*) and accessible via a continuous cycle footpath (part of the Celtic Trail; see *Walking, riding and cycling trails*), with a 1km seafront promenade, 250 acres of wetland habitat, and an 18-hole Jack Nicklaus golf course. **8 B5**

Pembrey Country Park *Pembrey/Pembre, Carmarthenshire* A country park comprising one of Britain's best beaches, an adventure play area, dry ski slope, toboggan ride, crazy golf, train ride and a variety of nature trails. www.pembreycountrypark.wales **8 B2**

Other natural features

Anglesey and Snowdonia

Aberffraw Heritage Coast *Aberffraw, Isle of Anglesey* A coastline with sand dunes up to 9 metres high, on the site of a silted-up estuary. The Llys Llewelyn Countryside Heritage Centre in Aberffraw has displays on local history and wildlife. **66 F4**

Bala Lake (Llyn Tegid) *Bala/Y Bala, Gwynedd* The largest natural body of water in Wales, at 7km in length and up to 1.5km wide, popular for watersports. Among its many species of fish is the very rare gwyniad, and there are steam trains along its southern shore. https://visitbala.org.uk **54 B3**

Bardsey Island/Ynys Enlli *Gwynedd* A small island and wildlife sanctuary about 2km off the eastern tip of the Llyn peninsula, also known as Enlli. It also has the remains of St Mary's Augustinian abbey and some farmhouses listed as Ancient Monuments. www.bardsey.org **50 D2**

Conwy Falls (Rhaeadr y Graig Lwyd) *Penmachno, Conwy* A waterfa providing a habitat for ducks, otters and crested newts, set in 9.5 acres of ancient woodland with 32 species of birds, polecats and more. **60 D3**

Glan y Môr Elias *Traeth Lafan, Llanfairfechan, Conwy* A saltmarsh attracting all manner of birdlife, particularly roosting seabirds. **68 D3**

Parys Mountain (Mynydd Parys) *Amlwch, Isle of Anglesey* A Site of Special Scientific Interest, with evidence of mining taking place as far back as the Bronze Age. **67 A5**

Penrhos Coastal Park *Holyhead/Caergybi, Isle of Anglesey* A rugged 8km stretch of coastline comprising woodland, farmland, beaches and mudflats and providing a home to a wide variety of birdlife. **66 C2**

Swallow Falls *Betws-y-Coed, Conwy* A series of dramatic waterfalls, considered one of the prettiest spots i North Wales. **60 C3**

Cardiff and Vale of Glamorgan

Merthyr Mawr Warren *Merthyr Mawr, Bridgend* One of Europe's largest areas of sand dunes, providing an important habitat for plants and wildlife and designated a Site of Speci Scientific Interest, with a network of footpaths. 'Lawrence of Arabia' was filmed here. **2 A4**

Mid Wales and Brecon Beacons

Dan Yr Ogof, National Showcaves Centre For Wales *halfway between Swansea and Brecon, Abercraf, Powys* An award-winning showcaves complex, the biggest in northern Europe, containing one of the world's largest dinosaur parks, a replica Iron Age farm, stone circles, a museum, farm animals, a shire horse centre and playgrounds. www.showcaves.co.uk **24 E1**

Elan Valley Estate *near Rhayader/Rhaeadr Gwy, Powys* A scenic area with abundant wildlife and a Visitor Centre with interactive resources www.elanvalley.org.uk **40 E4**

Radnor Forest Valley *New Radnor, Powys* A valley in the heart of rural mid Wales, with spectacular and unspoilt countryside (once a royal hunting ground). Activities include walking, riding and cycling, especially mountain biking. https://naturalresources.wales **42 E1**

North East Wales

Ceiriog Valley *Wrexham/Wrecsam, Wrexham* An unspoilt valley described by Lloyd George as 'a little bit of heaven on earth', once home to poets John 'Ceiriog' Hughes, Huw Morus an Rev. Robert Ellis. Crossed by the Offa's Dyke path and other footpaths and bridleways, including the former Glyn Valley Tramway. **55 A8**

Pistyll Rhaeadr *Wrexham* The highest waterfall in England and Wales, at 240ft. **55 C6**

Ruabon Mountain, World's End and Panorama Circular *Llangollen, Denbighshire* A spectacular outcrop of carboniferous limestone set with coral and seashell fossils, popular with walkers, climbers and picnickers. **63 E5**

Swansea, Gower and Vale of Neath

Aberdulais Falls *Aberdulais, Neath Port Talbot* A famous waterfall owned y the National Trust, with Europe's iggest electricity-generating aterwheel set amidst historic emains, plus interactive displays. www.nationaltrust.org.uk **10 C2**

liw Valley *east of, Pontarddulais, wansea* A valley with waterfalls, anquil woods and open moorland. ronze Age artifacts have been ound at Mynydd March Hywel near ontardawe and there was a strong oman presence around Loughor eucarum). **9 B7**

alleys of South Wales

wmcarn Forest *Cwmcarn, Caerphilly* forested area with an 11km drive ffording magnificent countryside iews. There are seven car parks, some ith BBQ sites, picnic spots, adventure layrounds and walking routes, a cenic campsite, and a Visitor Centre Nantgarw Road, Cwmcarn). **12 C4**

iarwnant Forest *Llwyn-on-village, Merthyr Tydfil* A forest area vith walking and off-road cycling outes (including a special route or disabled visitors), an adventure layground, interpretation boards, a isitor Centre and picnic sites. **25 E5**

irhowy Valley *near Crosskeys, Caerphilly* A woodland walking and ycling base containing former coal-arrying railway tracks (including the ecently restored Penllwyn Tramroad ridge, with original stone sleepers), he Flatwoods Meadows Local Nature eserve, climbs to Graig Goch Wood nd Twyn yr Oerfel for excellent iews, part of Route 47 of the National ycleway, and Ynys Hywel Farm, a aditional working hill farm. **12 D4**

West Wales

Bosherston Lily Ponds *Bosherston, Pembrokeshire* Three flooded mestone valleys renowned for their overing of lilies (best in June), set mong woodland and dunes and a ood place to see breeding heron and oodland and migrating birds. Owned y the National Trust, they are linked to road Haven beach (see *Beaches and esorts*) by a footpath. **17 F5**

Gwaun Valley *near Fishguard / Abergwaun, Pembrokeshire* A eep wooded valley considered by eologists one of the world's best xamples of sub-glacial meltwater hannels, with an abundance of vildlife and prehistoric sites, and the Cilrhedyn Woodland Centre. **19 B8** *Parks and gardens* Penlan Uchaf Gardens.

Lydstep Caverns *Lydstep Point, Pembrokeshire* National Trust sea aves, including Smuggler's Cave and he Droch, with steps and handrails. **17 E7**

Preseli Hills *Crymych, Pembrokeshire* Rolling moors popular with walkers, cyclists and horse-riders, with Neolithic urial chambers, Bronze Age cairns, tone circles, standing stones and on Age forts, plus panoramic views of the Wicklow Mountains in Ireland, Snowdonia, the Brecon Beacons, and he Bristol Channel and West Country. Walks include the 12km Golden Road, an ancient trackway that linked Celtic settlements, passing bluestone outcrops, sites linked with King Arthur, nd an abandoned hillfort. **20 A1**

Stack Rocks *near Bosherston, Pembrokeshire* An area with some of Britain's most dramatic coastal liff forms, including Elegug Stacks, wo detached limestone pillars with reeding colonies of guillemots Elegug is Welsh for guillemot), azorbills and kittiwakes, and the Green Bridge of Waves, a wave-carved rch. Nearby is St Govan's Chapel and Well (see *Religious buildings*). Access is via a road through an army firing range (sometimes closed). **17 F5**

Strumble Head *Pembrokeshire Coast National Park, near Goodwick / Wdig, Pembrokeshire* A magnificent headland with a lighthouse on a large rock connected to the mainland by a narrow bridge, a sheltered bird observatory, and views over beaches where seals rear their pups. In winter there are spectacular passages of manx shearwaters, gannets and kittiwakes, and it's the best place in the area to see tern and skuas. **19 A5**

Parks and gardens

See also *Houses and Gardens*.

Anglesey and Snowdonia

Bodnant Gardens *near Llandudno, Conwy* Late-19th-century gardens with views across to the Snowdonian mountains, divided into a series of Italianate terraces and the Deep Dell, traversed by the River Hiraethlyn. www.nationaltrust.org.uk **69 E5**

Happy Valley Park *Llandudno, Conwy* A Victorian park with a restored 1890 camera obscura, woodland walks, a tea pavilion and an entertainment centre. www.greatorme.co.uk **69 C5**

Cardiff and Vale of Glamorgan

Dyffryn Gardens *St Nicholas, Vale of Glamorgan* A 70-acre parkland with landscaped gardens with exotic plants, an arboretum and a tearoom. www.dyffryngardens.org.uk **4 B1**

Mid Wales and Brecon Beacons

Glanusk Park and Estate *Crickhowell / Crug Hywell, Powys* A vast estate on the site of a former ironmaster's mansion in Brecon Beacons / Bannau Brycheiniog National Park (see *National Parks and AONBs*), containing several listed historic structures, including Celtic standing stones, Tower Bridge over the River Usk, and a private chapel. It is also known for its many oak species. **26 D2**

Swansea, Gower and Vale of Neath

Brynmill Park *next to Singleton Park, Swansea / Abertawe, Swansea* A listed Victorian park with a pond with swans and ducks, ornamental plantings, a bowling green, a playground and children's events and activities in summer **9 D8**

Cwmdonkin Park *Black Pill, Swansea* A family park with formal and informal play areas, formal flower beds and a water garden with a memorial stone to Dylan Thomas (a regular visitor). **9 D7**

Plantasia *Swansea / Abertawe, Swansea* A hi-tech hothouse with one of Wales's best collections of plants, including giant bamboo, ferns and cacti, a butterfly house, a colony of cotton-top Tamarin monkeys, and a variety of insects, reptiles and fish. There are treasure trails and children's activities, and guided tours by prior request. **9 D8**

Singleton Park and Clyne Botanic Gardens *Sketty, Swansea* A large park containing a walled botanical complex with internationally recognised collections of rhododendrons, enkianthus and pieris, a bog garden, and scenic woodlands. **9 D7**

Valleys of South Wales

Bedwellty Park *Tredegar, Blaenau Gwent* A 26-acre Victorian park with period features, including an ice house, a grotto and an arboretum, and containing the biggest single block of coal ever cut (15 tons) and Bedwellty House, an ironmaster's residence built in 1818. **25 F7**

▲ **Clyne Park, Swansea**
Thierry Maffeis / Dreamstime

West Wales

Aberglasney Gardens *Llangathen, Carmarthenshire* Ten-acre gardens dating back to 1477, set in the attractive Tywi Valley and embracing two woodland areas. https://aberglasney.org **22 C4**

Begelly Park Gardens *Narberth Rd, Begelly, Pembrokeshire* Twelve-acre gardens, including a Japanese garden and water features, with a lakeside picnic area and an 18th-century tearoom.**17 C8**

Colby Woodland Gardens *near Amroth, Pembrokeshire* National Trust gardens in a secluded valley, with one of Wales's best collections of rhododendrons and azaleas, plus woodland trails and views over Carmarthen Bay. The gallery shows paintings, pottery, woodwork and crafts, primarily by local artists. www.nationaltrust.org.uk **20 F3**

Hilton Court Gardens *Roch, Pembroke-shire* A 9-acre area of woodland and lakes with craft workshops and a tearoom. **19 E5**

Manorowen Walled Garden *Fishguard / Abergwaun, Pembrokeshire* A small walled garden dating back to 1750, site of skirmish during the brief French invasion of Wales during the Napoleonic Wars, with a historic gazebo and resident sculptor. **19 B6**

National Botanic Garden of Wales *Llanarthne, Carmarthenshire* A world-class botanic showpiece opened in 2000, featuring a Japanese Garden with a stream, teahouse and cherry trees; a Theatr Botanica with a film celebrating the world of plants; lakeside and prairie walks; and water sculptures. Guided tours are available, and there are picnic areas and a children's playground and activities https://botanicgarden.wales **22 D3**

Norwood Gardens *Llanllwni, Carmarthenshire* A 3-acre garden begun in 2003 and still under development, with a Long Walk leading to seven circular themed gardens, including a bamboo garden, American colonial garden and alpine garden, and a tearoom. **32 D2**

Penlan Uchaf Gardens *near Fishguard / Abergwaun, Pembrokeshire* A 3-acre landscaped garden in the attractive Gwaun Valley (see *Other natural features*). **19 B8**

Upton Castle Gardens *near Cosheston, Pembrokeshire* Ground and gardens containing more than 250 species of trees and shrubs in a secluded wooded valley. www.uptoncastle.co.uk **17 D6**

Boat trips

See also Cardigan Bay Special Area of Conservation; Ceredigion Heritage and Marine Heritage Coast; Flat Holm Island; Ramsey Island RSPB Reserve; and Skomer, Skokholm and Grassholm (all *Nature reserves and conservation areas*); and also *Transport and Watersports*.

Anglesey and Snowdonia

Queen Victoria *Conwy Quay, Conwy, Conwy* Riverbus trips to the Conwy Valley or around the estuary to see Puffin Island, Anglesey and the Great Orme. **69 D5**

Cardiff and Vale of Glamorgan

Aquabus *Cardiff Bay Barrage, Penarth, Vale of Glamorgan* A waterbus service providing all-weather trips around Cardiff Bay. https://aquabus.co.uk **4 B3**

Waverley and Balmoral *Penarth Pier, Penarth, Vale of Glamorgan* Summer trips along the Welsh coast and to Somerset and Devon, including journeys in the world's last seagoing paddlesteamer. www.waverleyexcursions.co.uk **4 B3**

West Wales

Voyages of Discovery *1 High St, St David's / Tyddewi, Pembrokeshire* Guided marine tours of the inshore and offshore Pembrokeshire islands, run byconservationists. www.ramseyisland.co.uk **18 D3**

Animal attractions

See also Merlin's Hill (*Monuments and ancient sites*) and *Nature reserves and conservation areas*.

Anglesey and Snowdonia

Anglesey Sea Zoo *Brynsiencyn, Isle of Anglesey* Award-winning displays of marine life from the surrounding waters. www.angleseyseazoo.co.uk **67 F6**

Bodafon Farm Park *Llandudno, Conwy* A working farm with rare farm breeds, aviaries with owls and tropical birds, a heritage trail and miniature farm tractors. https://bodafonfarmpark.com **69 C5**

Pili Palas *Menai Bridge / Porthaethwy, Isle of Anglesey* A tropical environment with butterflies, exotic plants, birds, snakes and lizards, plus indoor play zone. www.pilipalas.co.uk **67 E8**

Welsh Mountain Zoo *Colwyn Bay / Bae Colwyn, Conwy* A conservation zoo in beautiful gardens above Colwyn Bay, with hundreds of animal and plant species from around the world. www.welshmountainzoo.org **69 D6**

Cardiff and Vale of Glamorgan

Cefn Mably Farm Park *off Began Rd, near St Mellons / Llaneurwg, Cardiff* A rural farm with rare breeds, animal petting, pony rides, toys and a picnic area. www.cefnmablyfarmpark.com **12 F4**

Warren Mill Farm Park *Pendoylan, near Cowbridge / Y Bont Faen, Vale of Glamorgan* A farm with rare and miniature farm animals and a four-acre lake. www.warrenmillfarm.co.uk **3 A7**

Mid Wales and Brecon Beacons

Kite Country *Gigrin Farm Feeding Station, South St, Rhayader, Rhayader / Rhaeadr Gwy, Powys* Several centres where visitors can view breeding red kites and other wildlife, including buzzards and ravens, in their natural environment. https://gigrin.co.uk **40 E4**

North East Wales

Rhyl Seaquarium *East Parade, Rhyl / Y Rhyl, Denbighshire* An aquarium with Wales's only walkthrough underwater tunnel, the Ocean Falls Cascade, the Sea at Night, with catfish and octopuses, and the Shark Encounter. www.seaquariumrhyl.co.uk **70 C2**

Swansea, Gower and Vale of Neath

Black Pill Wildlife Centre *Black Pill, Swansea* A feeding station for migratory waders, including sanderlings, ringed plovers and oystercatchers, and a Site of Special Scientific Interest **9 D7**

Valleys of South Wales

Fforest Uchaf Horse and Pony Rehabilitation Centre *Maindy Rd, Pencoedcae, Pontypridd, Rhondda Cynon Taff* A working farm and home to horses and ponies in need. **11 E8**

West Wales

Badger Watch *Dinefwr Park, Llandeilo, Carmarthenshire* A National Trust centre where visitors can observe badgers in their natural habitat. www.nationaltrust.org.uk **32 D3**

British Bird of Prey Centre *Manordeifi, near Llechryd, Ceredigion* A falconry centre where visitors can try setting birds free and commanding them back. www.britishbirdofpreycentre.co.uk **21 D3**

The Mumbles *The Mumbles / Y Mwmbwls, Swansea* A small, picturesque Victorian seaside resort, with a pier built in 1898, a lighthouse, award-winning family beaches (Bracelet Bay and Limeslade Bay), craf galleries, and the famous 'Mumbles Mile' of seafront pubs. **9 E7**
Walking, riding and cycling trails Swansea Bay Foreshore Path *Castles* Oystermouth Castle *Watersports* Gower Coast Adventure

Port Eynon and Horton *Port Eynon, Swansea* Two adjoining beaches with impressive stretches of golden sand. **8 E4** *Watersports* Gower Coast Adventures

Rhossili *Swansea* A stunning Nationa Trust beach with excellent bathing an spectacular views of Worms Head, a Welsh landmark. Access is via a steep path. **8 E3**

Swansea Bay *Swansea / Abertawe, Swansea* An 8km stretch of sand with promenade. **9 D8**

Tor Bay *Penmaen, Swansea* A fine National Trust beac a 1.5km walk from the village of Penmaen, wtih spectacular views from the neighbouring Great Tor headland. **9 E5**

West Wales

Abereiddy *Pembrokeshire* A beautifully sited coastal town with a sand and shingle bay famous for its 'Blue Lagoon', a flooded slate quarry. **18 C3**

Barafundle *Barafundle Bay, Bosherston, Pembrokeshire* A stunning unspoilt beach on the beautiful stretch of coastline around Stackpole and Bosherston, much of which is a National Trust estate, with lakes and circular walks. Nearby Stackpole Quay is one of Britain's smallest harbours. **17 F5**

Borth *Borth / Y Borth, Ceredigion* An old fishing hamlet with one of Ceredigion's longest beaches, with shallow waters popular with sailboarders and families. At certain times of year the tides reveal the stumps and trunks of ancient forests hidden beneath the sand. There is a footpath along the Ceredigion Heritage and Marine Heritage Coast (see *Nature reserves and conservation areas*) to Aberystwyth (see *Towns and villages*). **44 E3**

Broad Haven *Bosherston, Pembrokeshire* A large, popular and safe sandy beach with, at its northern extent, interesting geological features in the cliffs and excellent rock pools. A footpath leads to Bosherston Lily Pond (see *Other natural features*). **17 F5**

Cefn Sidan *near Kidwelly / Cydweli, Carmarthenshire* A multi-award-winning 12km beach fringed by sand dunes, with wonderful views over the Gower coastline. **8 B8**

Cwm-yr-Eglwys *Dinas Cross, Pembrokeshire* One of Wales's most attractive coves, with a wall and bellcote remaining from a church destroyed in the great storm of 1859. It can be reached on a spectacular circular walk from Pwllgwaelod cove around Dinas Island. **19 B8**

Dale *Pembrokeshire* A popular and attractive boating centre with competitive sailing and boarding in summer and an August regatta. **16 C2**
Watersports West Wales Wind Surf and Sail

Canolfan Y Barcud Kite Centre *Dewi Rd, Tregaron, Ceredigion* An information centre for red kites and other local wildlife, including that of Cors Goch Glan Teifi / Cors Caron (see *Nature reserves and conservation areas*), with live film of red kites, otters, owls, bats and small birds, and kite feeding in winter. It contains a small local history museum depicting life in rural communities, and a Welsh tearoom. **39 F6**

Cardigan Bay Marine Wildlife Centre *2nd Floor, Patent Slip, New Quay / Ceinewydd, Ceredigion* A research and public information centre about dolphins, seals and sea birds of Cardigan Bay and the Irish Sea, with interactive displays and a children's corner and activities.
www.cbmwc.org **31 A7**

Cardigan Island Coastal Farm Park *Gwbert, Ceredigion* A unique farm park on a headland overlooking the nature reserve of Cardigan Island just offshore, offering sightings of Atlantic grey seals (which breed in the caves below the park), bottlenose dolphins and rare choughs (which nest on the cliffs). Shetland ponies, Vietnamese pigs, rare breed cattle, and llamas also feature, plus special times when children may feed the animals. **30 C3**

Dyfed Shires and Leisure Farm *Carnhaun, Eglwyswrw, Pembrokeshire* A traditional farm offering pony and wagon rides, a museum, demonstrations, animal-feeding sessions, play areas and more. **30 E2**

Folly Farm Adventure Park *Begelly, Kilgetty, near Tenby / Dinbych-y-Pysgod, Pembrokeshire* The biggest farm attraction in Wales, with a childrens' zoo, petting and feeding sessions, milking and falconry displays, indoor and outdoor play areas, a vintage funfair and a magic show. **17 C8**

Manor House Wildlife and Leisure Park *St Florence, Pembrokeshire* A wild animal park with more than 200 species of mammals, birds, fish and reptiles. www.manorhousewildanimalpark.co.uk **17 D7**

National Wetlands Centre Wales *Penclacwydd, Llwynhendy, Llanelli, Carmarthenshire* An award-winning and innovative centre with ponds, lakes and reedbeds providing a habitat for thousands of ducks, swans and geese, and a Millennium Wetland complex

housing dragonflies, little egrets and more. **8 B5**

Ocean Lab *The Parrog, Goodwick / Wdig, Pembrokeshire* An aquarium with an exhibition gallery, hands-on activities relating to the sea and shore life, a simulated submarine journey through time, computer games, ocean-themed soft play and more. www.ocean-lab.co.uk **19 B6**

Red Kite Feeding Station *Cross Inn, Llanddeusant, Llangadog, Carmarthenshire* A feeding station attracting more than 30 red kites and buzzards daily, with a purpose-built hide (wheelchair accessible) holding up to 20 people.
www.redkiteswales.co.uk **23 C8**

Welsh Wildlife Centre *Cilgerran, Pembrokeshire* A large reed bed on the banks of the River Teifi, home to breeding reed, sedge and Cetti's warblers and more. There are hides, a futuristic Visitor Centre and a programme of family activities and regular events.
www.welshwildlife.org **30 D3**

Beaches and resorts

Anglesey and Snowdonia

Aberdaron *Gwynedd* An old fishing village with whitewashed houses, at the mouth of the river Daron, spanned by a 17-century stone bridge. There are heritage trails and a popular beach, and about 2km away Porthor Beach has sand that whistles when walked on. **50 C3**

Aberdyfi / Aberdovey *Gwynedd* A pretty little harbour resort within Snowdonia National Park, with award-winning beaches and an estuary with views of Cardigan Bay. Popular with watersports fans and golfers. **44 D3**

Abersoch *Gwynedd* A busy coastal resort and important sailing and surfing centre on Cardigan Bay, with the sandy beaches of Porth Fawr, Porth Bach and Porth Ceiriad. **51 C6**

Cemaes *Isle of Anglesey* The most northerly village on Anglesey, situated in an AONB and part of the 30km North Anglesey Heritage Coast, with a natural harbour that housed ancient settlements, a popular sheltered sandy beach and a Llanbadrig Church with its Muslim features (see *Religious buildings*). **66 A4**

Criccieth *Gwynedd* An attractive resort on the shores of Cardigan Bay, with the remains of a 1239 stone castle

(see *Castles*), a Lloyd George Museum (see *Local history*), a central green that was part of the medieval common, and sandy beaches drawing watersports enthusiasts. **52 A1**

Llanbedrog *Gwynedd* A village best known for its for its sheltered sandy beach beneath a heather-covered, pine-fringed headland, owned by the National Trust. Nearby is Mynydd Tir y Cwmwd mountain, with panoramic views, and Tremfan Hall, once home to scholar John Gwenogfryn Evans. **51 B6**

Llandudno *Conwy, Conwy* A Victorian seaside resort with a host of attractions, including a promenade, a pier (see *Family attractions*), two beaches and a cable car to the summit of the Great Orme headland (see *Outdoors: Country and forest parks*). **69 C5**

Newry Beach *Holyhead / Caergybi, Isle of Anglesey* A beach with the largest breakwater in Europe, a good marina and a promenade. **66 C2**

Porth Dinllaen *Gwynedd* An old fishing hamlet with a rich maritime history, a lifeboat station and a spectacularly sited golf course on the headland. The surrounding land was recently purchased by the National Trust. **58 F1**

Porth Trecastel *near Rhosneigr, Isle of Anglesey* Anglesey's best beach, set in a picturesque cove with clean water and excellent sand. **66 E3**

Porthmadog *Gwynedd* A harbour town on the Glaslyn Estuary, with a seafaring past, numerous craft shops and a beach, Blackrock Sands, on its outskirts. The Ffestiniog Railway (see *Transport*) starts here, TE Lawrence (of Arabia) lived nearby and the poet Shelley visited often. **52 A3**

Pwllheli *Gwynedd* A characterful coastal market town with narrow streets, a historic harbour, a Blue Flag beach, Hafan Pwllheli Marina (see *Watersports*), Plas Glyn y Weddw Art Gallery (see *Art and crafts*) and Pennarth Fawr, a medieval stone house with a wooden interior. **51 A7**

Rhosneigr *Isle of Anglesey* A popular resort with award-winning beaches: Traeth Crigyll (Town Beach), a magnet for windsurfers and sailors; and Broad Beach, a venue for canoeing, surfing and walking. **66 E3**

Cardiff and Vale of Glamorgan

Barry Island *Vale of Glamorgan* A traditional seaside resort with the long, sheltered, sandy beach of Whitmore Bay with its rock pools, a promenade, amusement arcades and a funfair. **4 C2** *Transport* Barry Island Railway Heritage Centre *Family attractions* Barry Island Pleasure Park

Penarth *Vale of Glamorgan* A resort town with a restored Victorian pier offering trips in a seagoing paddlesteamer (see *Boat trips*) and a modern marina. **4 B3** *Country, coastal and forest parks* Cosmeston Lakes Country Park *Local history* Cosmeston Medieval Village *Science and technology* Cardiff Bay Barrage

Porthcawl *Bridgend* South Wales's most popular seaside resort, with miles of unspoiled sand stretching across three bays, Rest Bay, Sandy Bay and Tresco Bay. **2 A3**
Nature reserves and conservation areas Glamorgan Heritage Coast
Military history Porthcawl Museum

North East Wales

Barkby Beach, Central Beach and Ffrith Beach *near Prestatyn, Denbighshire* Three sandy beaches joined by a 7km promenade that has been incorporated into the National Cycle Network and has spectacular views of Snowdonia, Anglesey and the Wirral. The award-winning Central marks the start of the Offa's Dyke Trail (see *Walking, cycling and riding trails*). **70 C3**

Swansea, Gower and Vale of Neath

Aberavon *Neath Port Talbot* A safe, sandy 3km beach with a promenade for walking and cycling (part of the National Cycle Network Route 4 along the south Wales coast), an area of unspoilt dunes, and excellent views over Swansea Bay and the Devon coast. **10 D2**
Family attractions Aquadome

Caswell Bay *Caswell, Swansea* A very pretty bay popular with families and good for watersports. **9 E6**

Langland Bay *The Mumbles / Y Mwmbwls, Swansea* An excellent sandy beach popular with watersports enthusiasts and families, with distinctive striped beach huts. **9 E7**

Llangennith *Rhossili, Swansea* One of the best surf beaches in the country. **8 E3**

Towns and villages

See also Beaches and Resorts

See also Beaches and Resorts

Anglesey and Snowdonia

Beddgelert *Gwynedd* An award-winning mountain village at the confluence of the Glaslyn and Colwyn rivers, where Alfred Bestall wrote Rupert the Bear stories and Prince Llywelyn had a cottage (visitors can see the grave of Gelert, the dog left by Llywelyn to guard his child). **59 E7**
Local history & industry Sygun Copper Mine

Betws-y-coed *Conwy* The main village of the Snowdonia National Park and North Wales's most popular inland resort, with many craft and outdoor activity shops. Popular in Victorian times as an artists' colony. **60 C3**
Country & forest parks Gwydyr Forest Park *Other natural features* Swallow Falls *Walking, cycling and riding trails* Marin Trails

Capel Curig *Conwy* A rugged mountain village at the heart of Snowdonia National Park, popular with climbers and walkers. **60 C2**
Climbing and caving Plas-y-Brenin National Mountain Centre *Houses and gardens* The Ugly House

Conwy *Conwy* One of the best-preserved walled towns in Europe, containing the 'smallest house in Britain' (6ft x 10ft). Nearby Gwydyr Forest and Coed y Brenin Forest are good for walks. **69 D5**
Art and crafts Royal Cambrian Academy *Buildings* Aberconwy House • Conwy Castle • Plas Mawr *Museums* Teapot World *Local history and industry* Conwy Mussel Museum *Outdoors* Conwy Butterfly Jungle • Queen Victoria Boat Trips *Transport* Conwy Suspension Bridge

Llanfairpwllgwyngyllgogery-chwyrndrobwllllantysiliogogogoch *Isle of Anglesey* The town with perhaps the world's most-photographed railway-station sign. Also the Marquis of Anglesey's Column dating back to 1816 and panoramic views of Anglesey and Snowdonia. **67 E7**

Portmeirion *near Porthmadog, Gwynedd* An Italianate village created by architect Sir Clough Williams-Ellis from 1925 to 1975 and made famous by the cult 1960s show 'The Prisoner'. **52 A3**

Rhiw *Gwynedd* One of the highest villages on the Llyn peninsula, with some of the best views in Wales and much evidence of early settlement, including dolmens, early field patterns and the site of a Stone Age axe-head 'factory'. **50 C4**
Houses and gardens Plas yn Rhiw

Trefriw *Conwy* A village skirted by an ancient Roman road, with the still-operational Trefriw Wells, a spa used by the Romans. A one-time river port and then a tourist centre, it retains some large Victorian houses that began life as boarding houses, and also boasts a wool mill. **60 B3**

Cardiff and Vale of Glamorgan

Llantwit Major *Llantwit Major/Llanilltud Fawr, Vale of Glamorgan* An historic town close to the Glamorgan Heritage Coast (see *Nature reserves and conservation areas*), with narrow streets and picturesque stone cottages, plus the remains of Iron Age hillforts and a Roman villa, Celtic crosses, a medieval grange and impressive Tudor buildings. **3 C6**
Castles St Donats Castle *Religious buildings* St Illtud's Church

Merthyr Mawr *Bridgend* A delightful village on the edge of Merthyr Mawr Warren (see *Other natural features*), surrounded by woods and meadows. It has thatched cottages, a 15th-century inn and a 19th-century church built on an ancient worship site. **2 A4**
Castles Candleston Castle

Mid Wales and Brecon Beacons

Berriew *Powys* A charming little village with traditional black-and-white Welsh houses, frequently voted Best Kept Village in Wales and set in beautiful countryside. **47 C7**
Art and crafts Andrew Logan Museum of Sculpture

Brecon *Brecon/Aberhonddu, Powys* A 12th-century town founded just east of a Norman castle marking the original settlement, with several towers and gateways remaining from the 13th-century defensive walls and the Usk Bridge dating from 1563. **25 B5**
Walking, riding and cycling trails Taff Trail • Usk Valley Walk *Animal*

---

eshwater East and West
eshwater East, Pembrokeshire A retty, dune-backed sandy beach with holiday centre, and, to the west, in n isolated location, Wales's most onsistent surfing beach. **17 E6**
ctivity centres Fresh Adventure

ittle Haven *Pembrokeshire* A popular llage between high cliffs, with onvivial inns surrounding a sandy each. **16 B3**

Manorbier *Manorbier/Maenorbŷr, embrokeshire* A pretty seaside llage with an impressive sandy ove popular with surfers, a Norman hurch, a restored beerhouse and the ing's Quoit, a stone cromlech on the oastal path. The birthplace of Gerald f Wales, it was a favourite retreat of eorge Bernard Shaw and Virginia Voolf. **17 E7**
Castles Manorbier Castle

Marloes Sands *Marloes, embrokeshire* A spectacular and solated southwest-facing beach with ocky outcrops, owned by the National rust. ⬚ www.nationaltrust.org.uk **6 C1**

ewgale Beach *Newgale, embrokeshire* A splendid 3km beach acked by a huge pebble stormbank, opular with surfers and windsurfers.

Traces of a submerged prehistoric forest are occasionally exposed by low spring tides.

New Quay/Ceinewydd *Ceredigion* A former shipbuilding centre and commercial port, now a popular sailing centre and resort among Welsh holidaymakers, with Ceredigion Heritage and Marine Heritage Coast paths (see *Nature reserves and conservation areas*) leading to the south and north. **18 E5**
Walking, riding and cycling trails Dylan Thomas Ceredigion Trail *Animal attractions* Cardigan Bay Marine Wildlife Centre *Local history* Amgueddfa Ceredigion Cei Newydd *Riding* Cwntydu Riding and Trekking Centre

Saundersfoot *Pembrokeshire* A charming former fishing village and resort with a scenic harbour and wide beach popular with watersports enthusiasts. **17 D8**
Walking, riding and cycling trails Miners' Way

Tenby *Tenby/Dinbych-y-Pysgod, Pembrokeshire* A delightful old walled town with three award-winning

beaches, a picturesque harbour and panoramic views across Carmarthen from Castle Hill **17 D8**
Walking, riding and cycling trails Celtic Trail *Animal attractions* Silent World Aquarium and Reptile Collection *Castles* Tenby Castle *Houses and gardens* Tudor Merchant's House *Religious buildings* Caldey Abbey *Local history* Tenby Museum and Art Gallery

Traeth Penbryn *Llanerchaeron, Ciliau Aeron, Ceredigion* A sandy beach managed by the National Trust, accessible via the wooded Hoffnant Valley (which has a 1km woodland trail) and offering splendid views of Cardigan Bay. At low tide it is possible to walk as far as Tresaith (see below). **31 B5**

Tresaith *Ceredigion* A popular picture-postcard seaside village with an excellent sandy beach onto which the River Saith cascades from the cliff-tops. It is linked by a Ceredigion Heritage and Marine Heritage Coast path (see *Nature reserves and conservation areas*) to neighbouring Aberporth. **31 B5**

▼ **Porth Dinllaen**
Andy Chisholm / Dreamstimec

▼ **Portmeirion**
Xantana / Dreamstime

Devil's Bridge / Pontarfynach
Ceredigion A famous village in the foothills of the Pumlumon Mountains with waterfalls on the River Mynach and other stunning scenery, as well as three bridges built one one on top of the other; the first is believed to have been built by the Cistercian monks of Abaty Ystrad Fflur (see *Religious buildings*) or by the Knights Templar. **39 C7**
Transport Vale of Rheidol (Cwm Rheidol) Railway.

Eglwyswrw *Pembrokeshire* A medieval village with the remnants of motte-and-bailey fortification. **30 E2**
Monuments and ancient sites Castell Henllys

Fishguard and Goodwick
Fishguard / Abergwaun, Pembrokeshi Adjoining towns set around Fishguard Harbour, a good place for birdwatching, with picturesque quayside cottages in the Lower Town and good shops and galleries. **19 B7**
Walking, riding and cycling trails Celtic Trail • Last Invasion Trail *Animal attractions* Ocean Lab *Parks and gardens* Manorowen Walled Garden *Food & drink* Langloffan Farmhouse

Haverfordwest *Haverfordwest / Hwlffordd, Pembrokeshire* An attractive ancient county town with redeveloped quayside buildings and the recently excavated remnants of a Augustinian priory. **16 A4**
Walking, riding and cycling trails Withybush Woods
Castles Haverfordwest Castle
Family attractions Clerkenhill Farm Adventure

Laugharne *Laugharne / Talacharn, Carmarthenshire* A delightful town famous for its connection with Dylan Thomas, with a castle and views over the Taf Estuary. **21 E6**
Religious buildings St Martin
Historic buildings Dylan Thomas Boathouse and Writing Shed

Lawrenny *Pembrokeshire* An attractive village with a fine church, a picnic area on the site of the former castle, with wonderful river views, and a quay with a yachting and watersport centre and a popular inn. **17 C6**

Llandeilo *Carmarthenshire* A pretty historic town with narrow streets and Wales's biggest single-span stone bridge. **23 C5**

---

attractions Trefeinon Open Farm *Castles* Brecon Castle *Religious buildings* Brecon Cathedral *Local history* Brecknock Museum and Art Gallery *Military history* South Wales Borderers Museum *Transport* Brecon and Monmouthshire Canal • Water Folk Canal Centre *Riding* Cantref Riding Centre

Hay on Wye *Hay on Wye / Y Gelli Gandryll, Powys* The world's first 'book town', founded in 1961 on the Welsh-English border beneath the Black Mountains and containing almost 40 secondhand bookshops. It is dominated by a semi-restored castle, and the surrounding countryside is popular for walking, pony-trekking, hang-gliding and other open-air sports **36 D2**

Llandrindod Wells *Llandrindod Wells / Llandrindod, Powys* Britain's smallest town, the county town of Powys, and a popular base among mountain-bikers, cyclists, walkers and birdwatchers, set in the spectacular valley between the Cambrian Mountains (see *National Parks and AONBs*) and the Mynydd Epynt. A former spa town (there is still a medicinal spa in historic Rock Park), it is host to a Victorian festival each August and has the remains of a Roman fort. **41 F6**
Local history Radnorshire Museum
Transport National Cycle Collection

Welshpool *Welshpool / Y Trallwng, Powys* A town first mentioned in 1253, when it was protected by a timber castle on an earth mound (near the train station). An early-20th-century narrow-gauge railway runs from the top of town to Llanfair Caereinion, and every Monday one of Europe's biggest sheep markets is held here. **47 B8**
Walking, riding & cycling trails Glyndwr's Way *Nature reserves & conservation areas* Llyn Coed Y Dinas • Severn Farm Pond *Castles* Powis Castle *Local history* Powysland Museum and Montgomery Canal Centre

North East Wales
Bangor-is-y-coed (Bangor-on-Dee)
Bangor-is-y-coed, Wrexham A picturesque village accessed via a part-medieval, part-17th-century bridge (a scheduled Ancient Monument), once the site of an important monastery and now home to a country racecourse. **63 E8**

Corwen *Denbighshire* A quaint market town in the Vale of Edeyrnion,

at the foot of the Berwyn Mountains, often described as the 'crossroads of North Wales's because it forms a good base for touring. Overlooked by Caer Drewyn, an Iron Age hillfort. **62 F2**
Religious buildings Llangar Church • Rug Chapel

Denbigh *Denbigh / Dinbych, Denbighshire* An old market town with steep streets, two ruined churches, the early 14th-century church of St Hilary's, a Carmelite friary, the remnants of town walls and an ancient market. **62 A1**
Buildings Denbigh Castle • Leicester's Church

Holywell *Holywell / Treffynon, Flintshire* A quaint, slow-paced historic town with more than 60 listed buildings and specialist shops. **71 D5**
Country and forest parks Greenfield Valley Heritage and Country Park
Religious buildings St Winefride's Well

Llangollen *Denbighshire* A small town dating back to the 7th century, with the famous Dee Bridge (a scheduled Ancient Monument), some old mill sluice gates and the remains of a weir. **62 F5**
Buildings Castell Dinas Bran • Plas Newydd • Valle Crucis Abbey
Family attractions Llangollen Exhibition Centre • Victorian School of the 3 R's and Heritage Centre
Transport Llangollen Motor Museum • Llangollen Railway

Ruthin *Ruthin / Rhuthun, Denbighshire* A picturesque hilltop town with half-timbered buildings and medieval street; King Arthur is reputed to have had a love-rival executed at the 'Maen Huail' stone in front of Exmewe Hall. **62 C3**
Art and crafts Ruthin Craft Centre Gallery *Country and forest parks* Moel Famau Country Park
Local history and industry Old Gaol

St Asaph *St Asaph / Llanelwy, Denbighshire* An prominent town, with the 16th-century Bishops Palace, two old deaneries, some 1680 almshouses and the 1840 workhouse where HM Stanley of 'Doctor Livingstone, I presume' fame, spent his early years. **70 E2** *Religious buildings* St Asaph Cathedral

▶ Pembroke *Nicola Pulham / Dreamstime*

West Wales
Aberaeron *Ceredigion* One of Wales's first 'planned' towns, established in the 19th century, with a stonewalled, yacht-filled harbour dating back to its days as a thriving port. Quarter of the town's buildings are listed as being of special architectural or historical interest. **38 F2**
Walking, riding and cycling trails Dylan Thomas Ceredigion Trail *Animal attractions* Aberaeron Sea Aquarium *Food & drink* Gwinllan Ffynnon Las Vineyard *Family attractions* Family Golf Aberaeron

Aberystwyth *Ceredigion* A town established more than 700 years ago by a charter awarded by Edward I, surrounded on three sides by glorious British countryside, the Plynlimon mountains and the Rheidol Valley. **38 B4**
Nature reserves and conservation areas Ceredigion Heritage and Marine Heritage Coast *Castles* Aberystwyth Castle *Historic buildings* Great Aberystwyth Camera Obscura and Victorian Tearooms *Local history* Amgueddfa Ceredigion Aberystwyth • Llyfrgell Genedlaethol Cymru (National Library of Wales) *Transport*

Aberystwyth Rheilffordd Craig Glaid (Electric Cliff Railway) • Vale of Rheidol (Cwn Rheidol) Railway *Art and crafts* Canolfan Y Celfyddydau Aberystwyth Arts Centre

Angle *Pembrokeshire* A delightful village between two bays, with a long seafaring tradition, a lifeboat station and a medieval fortified residence, the Tower House. A good starting point for circular coastal walks. **16 D3**

Burton *Pembrokeshire* An attractive boating village with a landing pontoon and a pleasant waterside pub with a beer garden. **17 C5**

Carew *Pembrokeshire* A popular village at the end of a lovely tidal inlet of the Daugleddau Estuary, with a picnic site. **17 D6**
Castles Carew Castle *Monuments and ancient sites* Carew Cross *Factories, mills and mines* Carew Tidal Mill

Cenarth *Ceredigion* An interesting and scenic village with a famous salmon leap on the waterfall on the River Teifi, good riverside walks, a 17th-century flour mill and historic inns. **31 D5**
Local history National Coracle Centre.

nimal attractions Badger Watch ***ouses and gardens*** Newton House

andovery *Llandovery/Llanymddyfri, armarthenshire* An Upper Towy Valley arket town in a good walking country n the edge of the Brecon Beacons ational Park, with a ruined castle ith a monument commemorating ewelyn ap Gruffydd Fychan of Caeo, xecuted in 1401 for refusing to betray e cause of Welsh freedom, and the mnants of a Roman fort containing a edieval church. **33 F8**

andysul *Ceredigion* A Teifi Valley own popular with anglers and hitewater canoeists, with many ater-driven flour and woollen mills, e latter famous for their tapestries. earby Ffostrasol hosts Britain's ggest annual Celtic folk festival, Gwyl erin Y Cnapan. **31 D8** ***ocal history*** Amgueddfa Ceredigion andysul

angrannog *Ceredigion* A cturesque village with a spectacular alk leading up beyond hidden ilborth beach and around the eadland of National Trust owned Ynys ochtyn. **31 B6** ***Valking, riding and cycling trails*** ylan Thomas Ceredigion Trail

arberth *Narberth/Arberth, embroke-shire* A busy little market own that was home to the Welsh rinces of Dyfed in the Dark Ages, ith a ruined castle (currently being estored but open to visitors in ummer) **20 E2** ***nimal attractions*** Heron's Brook eisure Park ***Local history*** Wilson useum ***Art and crafts*** Queens all Gallery

ewport *Newport/Trefdraeth, embrokeshire* A delightful seafaring own with a 13th-century castle (now private residence), good watersports eaches (Newport Sands and Parrog), oetan Arthur prehistoric burial hamber, and art and crafts galleries. **9 B9** ***Monuments and ancient sites*** Carn ngli • Pentre Ifan Burial Chamber

embroke *Pembroke/Penfro, embrokeshire* A charming walled own dating back more than 900 years, vith many fine Georgian buildings, a ill pond with water birds and otters, nd a Visitor Centre recounting the own's history **17 D5** ***Castles*** Pembroke Castle ***ocal history*** Museum of the Home ***Military history*** Gun Tower

orthgain *Pembrokeshire* A 19th-nd early-20th-century seaport with n impressive harbour with restored uildings, fishing boats and yachts. **8 C4**

t David's *St David's/Tyddewi, embrokeshire* Britain's atmospheric mallest city and the birthplace of Vales's patron saint, with a splendid urfing beach (Whitesand Bay), a burial hamber and fortification at St David's Head, and the massive outcrop of Carn Llidi, with Britain's oldest rocks (6 million years old). **18 D3** ***Walking, riding and cycling trails*** Celtic Trail ***Boat trips*** Voyages of Discovery ***Religious buildings*** St David's Bishops Palace • St David's Cathedral • St Nons

St Florence *Pembrokeshire* An attractive village with pretty cottages, one of which boasts the area's last surviving Flemish chimney, plus a 13th-century church. **17 D7** ***Animal Attractions*** Manor Widlife Park ***Food and drink*** St Florence

Wye Valley and Vale of Usk

Abergavenny *Abergavenny/Y Fenni, Monmouthshire* An ancient market town, established on the site of the Roman fort of Gobannium, that grew alongside its Norman castle built in 1087. Among its many surviving original buildings are a Benedictine priory and houses in Nevill Street and Market Street. **26 E4** ***Castles*** Abergavenny Castle ***Local history*** Abergavenny Museum ***Food and drink*** Sugar Loaf Vineyard

Chepstow *Chepstow/Cas-Gwent, Monmouthshire* An historic walled border town in the Wye Valley AONB (see *National Parks and AONBs*), with a river walk with spectacular views, and a Victorian cast-iron road bridge. **14 D2** ***Castles*** Chepstow Castle ***Local history*** Chepstow Museum ***Horseracing*** Chepstown Racecourse

Monmouth *Monmouth/Trefynwy, Monmouthshire* An ancient market and border town that has retained its medieval street plan and 13th-century bridge gate, the only one in Britain with a fortified gatehouse. **27 E8** ***Castles*** Monmouth Castle ***Local history*** Local History Centre ***Military history*** Royal Monmouthshire Royal Engineers Regimental Museum

►**Harlech Castle** Valerijs Jegorovs/Dreamstime

Buildings

Castles

Anglesey and Snowdonia

Beaumaris Castle *Castle Street, Beaumaris, Isle of Anglesey* An unfinished castle intended as one of Edward I's 'iron ring', with an ingenious symmetrical concentric design involving four successive lines of fortifications. **68 D2**

Caernarfon Castle *Beaumaris, Isle of Anglesey* A commanding castle begun in 1283 as Edward I's seat of government and royal palace, with unique polygonal towers and colour-banded masonry. **59 B5**

Conwy Castle *Conwy, Conwy* A ruin considered to have been one of the greatest European fortresses, built by Edward I and accessed via an 1826 suspension bridge preserved by the National Trust. **69 D5**

Criccieth Castle *Castle Street, Criccieth, Gwynedd* A North Wales landmark on a headland between two beaches, originally a stronghold of the Welsh princes but annexed and extended by Edward I. 🖳www.cadw.gov.wales **52 A2**

Dolwyddelan Castle *Dolwyddelan, Conwy* A dramatically sited castle built by Welsh prince Llwelyn the Great in 1210-40, with a rectangular stone tower restored in Victorian times. **60 D2**

Gwydir Castle *Llanrwst, Conwy* A Tudor courtyard house built c.1500, using material from the dissolved medieval Abbey of Maenan, and containing a 1640s panelled dining room reclaimed from the New York Metropolitan Museum. The 10-acre garden is Grade I listed. 🖳www.gwydircastle.co.uk **60 B4**

Harlech Castle *Castle Square, Harlech, Gwynedd* A spectacularly sited castle built by Edward I in the late 13th century as part of his 'iron ring' and later taken by Welsh leader Owain Glyn Dwr as the seat of his parliament, with a twin-towered gatehouse and stunning views from its battlements. 🖳www.cadw.gov.wales **52 B3**

Penrhyn Castle *Bangor, Gwynedd* An exuberant early-19th-century neo-Norman castle built by a local slate and sugar baron, with a one-ton slate bed made for Queen Victoria and paintings by the likes of Rembrandt, Gainsborough and Canaletto. The stable block has two railway museums, a doll museum and two galleries. 🖳www.nationaltrust.org.uk **68 E2**

Cardiff and Vale of Glamorgan

Beaupre Castle *near St Hilary, Vale of Glamorgan* A castle later turned into an Elizabethan manor house, much rebuilt in the 16th century; the outer gatehouse and storeyed porch from that time are well preserved, and the 14th-century hall retains its heraldic fireplace. **3 B7**

Candleston Castle *Merthyr Mawr, Bridgend* The remains of a 15th-century fortified manor house inhabited by the powerful de Cantelupe family until the 19th century, surrounded by Merthyr Mawr Warren (see *Other natural features*). **2 A4**

Cardiff Castle (Castel Caerdydd) *Castle St, Cardiff/Caerdydd, Cardiff* A 2,000-year-old castle in the city centre, with Roman walls and a Norman keep. The spectacular late-19th-century interiors include Mediterranean and Arab themed rooms, and the grounds have free-roaming peacocks, geese and ducks. Inside are the Regimental Museum of Dragon Guards, Regimental Museum Royal Regiment of Wales and Welch Regiment Museum (see *Military history*). 🖳www.cardiffcastle.com **4 A3**

Castell Coch *Tongwynlais, Cardiff* A Victorian version of a medieval Welsh chieftain's stronghold, built for the Marquis of Bute on the site of a 13th-century castle, with fantastical interiors. **12 F2**

Coity Castle *near Bridgend/Pen-y-Bont ar Ogwr, Bridgend* The extensive remains of an important Norman powerbase, largely rebuilt in the 14th century, with a surviving gatehouse and curtain walls. **11 F5**

Fonmon Castle *Barry/Y Barri, Vale of Glamorgan* The remains of a medieval castle, one of the few still lived in as a home, with a rectangular keep surrounded by post-medieval wings. The drawing room, library, kitchen, walled gardens and woodlands are open to visitors. 🖳www.cadw.gov.wales **3 C7**

St Donats Castle *Llantwit Major/Llanilltud Fawr, Vale of Glamorgan* A medieval castle restored by US newspaper magnate William Randolph Hearst, with a number of fine original features. A summer retreat for Charlie Chaplin, Bing Crosby and the like, it's now home to a college but there are guided tours in summer and an art gallery with exhibitions featuring local, national and international artists. **3 C6**

St Quentin's Castle *Llanblethian, Vale of Glamorgan* A largely ruined 12th-century castle with an imposing 14th-century gatehouse, subject to ongoing restoration work. 🖳www.cadw.gov.wales **3 B6**

Mid Wales and Brecon Beacons

Brecon Castle *Brecon/Aberhonddu, Powys* A castle with its origins in a Norman castle built by Bernard de Neufmarche following the defeat of the Welsh in 1093, with a tower rebuilt in stone in the 12th century and surviving today as Bishop Ely's Tower. Part of the 13th-century Great Hall is still intact (now part of the Castle Hotel). **25 B5**

Montgomery Castle *Montgomery/Trefaldwyn, Powys* A ruined castle with its origins in a 1223 fortress built by Henry III of England to counter Llywelyn ap Gruffudd, Prince of Wales, rebuilt in stone by 1234. The surviving defences comprise a barbican, wide outer ditch, narrow inner ditch and the middle and inner wards. **47 D8**

Powis Castle *Welshpool/Y Trallwng, Powys* A National Trust-owned castle built in the 13th century by the last native prince of Powys and reconstructed as a grand country house in the 16th century, set around a large courtyard overlooking Italianate terraces and extensive gardens. Inside are Indian art and curiosities collected by Clive of India, a former owner. 🖳www.nationaltrust.org.uk **47 B8**

Tretower Castle and Court *Crickhowell/Crug Hywell, Powys* A castle with its origins in a wooden tower built on a motte, replaced by a stone keep, hall and other rooms in 1150 and altered in the 13th century, when the surviving three-storey round tower was built. In the 14th century a new house was built around a courtyard, of which there are remnants. Audio tours are available. 🖳www.cadw.gov.wales **26 C1**

North East Wales

Castell Dinas Bran *near Llangollen, Denbighshire* The medieval hilltop ruin of 'Crow Castle', 13th-century home of Madoc ap Gruffydd Maelor, founder of Valle Crucis Abbey, is surrounded by the remnants of an Iron Age hillfort and ditch and offers breathtaking views. **62 F5**

Chirk Castle *Chirk, Wrexham* A 1310 Marcher fortress, still home to the Myddelton family, with staterooms filled with Adam-style furniture, tapestries and portraits. The grounds include a thatched 'Hawk House', a classical pavilion, a 17th-century lime tree avenue and 18th-century parkland. 🖳www.nationaltrust.org.uk **56 A2**

Denbigh Castle *Denbigh/Dinbych, Denbighshire* A ruined hilltop castle with a triple-towered gatehouse, built as part of Edward I's 13th-century campaigns against the Welsh. 🖳www.cadw.gov.wales **62 A1**

Rhuddlan Castle *Rhuddlan, Denbighshire* A concentrically planned castle, the second of Edward I's 'iron ring', with a massive twin-towered gatehouse and diamond-shaped inner ward constructed in 1277. One side of its defences is formed by a protected dock dug out to allow ships access. 🖳www.cadw.gov.wales **70 D2**

Swansea, Gower and Vale of Neath

Oystermouth Castle *The Mumbles/Y Mwmbwls, Swansea* A fine, well-preserved castle on a small hill with excellent views over Swansea Bay, originally founded by William de Londres in the early 1100s. Most of what remains dates from a 13th-century stone rebuilding, and there is an early-14th-century chapel block. **9 E7**

Swansea Castle *Swansea/Abertawe, Swansea* A ruined clifftop castle, viewable only from the exterior. Originally a motte-and-bailey Norman castle first recorded in 1116, it was rebuilt in the early 13th century. The present remains are from the 'new castle' dating from the late 13th to early 14th century. 🖳www.cadw.gov.wales **9 D8**

Weobley Castle *Llanrhidian, Swansea* The substantial remains of a castle on a site fortified since at least 1304, with an exhibition on the story of Weobley and other historic sites on the Peninsula. 🖳www.cadw.gov.wales **8 D4**

Valleys of South Wales

Caerphilly Castle *Castle St, Caerphilly/Caerffili, Caerphilly* One of western Europe's greatest medieval castles, the biggest castle in Britain after Windsor, and the country's first truly concentric castle, built in the late 13th century by one of Henry III's most powerful barons and a masterpiece of military planning. There is a leaning tower, and an impressive inner ward with an exhibition on Welsh castles. 🖳www.cadw.gov.wales **12 E3**

West Wales

Aberystwyth Castle *Aberystwyth, Ceredigion* One of several castles built in Wales by Edward I to subdue the Welsh, constructed in

Historic buildings

Anglesey and Snowdonia

South Stack Lighthouse *Holyhead/Caergybi, Isle of Anglesey* A spectacular lighthouse on Holy Island, built in 1809 and accessed via 543 steps. The Visitor Centre, Ellin's Tower, has live footage of birds nesting on the cliffs. www.trinityhouse.co.uk **66 C1**

Mid Wales and Brecon Beacons

Judge's Lodging *Shire Hall, Broad St, Presteigne/Llanandras, Powys* A restored judge's apartments and his servants' quarters with original furnishings, along with the courtroom and cells; an audio tour accompanies visits. www.judgeslodging.org.uk **42 F4**

Swansea, Gower and Vale of Neath

Patti Pavilion *Swansea/Abertawe, Swansea* The former Winter Garden of Craig y Nos (see *Parks and gardens*), donated to Swansea by opera singer Dame Adelina Patti in 1918 and transported to the park. **9 D8**

Valleys of South Wales

Blaenavon Workmens' Hall *101 High St, Blaenavon, Torfaen* An impressive 1895 valleys miners' institute, now housing an auditorium and cinema. www.torfaen.gov.uk **26 F3**

Joseph Parry's Cottage *Chapel Row, Merthyr Tydfil/Merthyr Tudful, Merthyr Tydfil* A restored ironworker's house, part of a row built by the Cyfarthfa Iron Company, and the birthplace and childhood home of composer Dr Joseph Parry in the 1840s, with an exhibition about his life and works. In front is a small restored section of the Glamorganshire Canal, which linked Merthyr Tydfil ironworks to the docks at Cardiff. www.blaenau-gwent.gov.uk **25 F6**

Ty Mawr and Roundhouse Towers *Nantyglo, Blaenau Gwent* The foundations of Ty Mawr Mansion, built in 1816 for local ironmaster brothers, plus the surviving towers (viewable from the road only) of a fortress built to protect them in the event of a workers' uprising. www.blaenau-gwent.gov.uk **26 E1**

West Wales

Dylan Thomas Boathouse and Writing Shed *Dylans Walk, Laugharne/Talacharn, Carmarthenshire* The house where the poet spent the last four years of his life and where he wrote Under Milk Wood, now a Heritage Centre with displays, books, a tearoom and picnic areas. www.dylanthomasboathouse.com **21 E6**

Great Aberystwyth Camera Obscura and Victorian Tearooms *Constitution Hill, Cliff Terrace, Aberystwyth, Ceredigion* A reconstructed Victorian amusement on the hill overlooking Aberystwyth and Cardigan Bay, with a huge lens system focusing detailed views onto a screen in a darkened gallery and reached by cliff railway. www.visitmidwales.co.uk **38 B4**

Penrhos Cottage *near Maenclochog, Pembrokeshire* A preserved thatched cottage or 'Ty Unos', a type of house unique to Pembrokeshire, built overnight on land claimed 'as far as a stone could be thrown'. By appointment only. www.visitmidwales.co.uk **20 B1**

▲ Carreg Cennen Castle
Leighton Collins / Dreamstime

1277, rebuilt in 1282, and blown up by Cromwell's army in 1649. An original castle built by invading Norman forces was south of the existing ruins. **38 B4**

Carew Castle *Carew, Pembrokeshire* A fine castle by the town millpond, built as a Norman stonghold and converted into a Elizabethan manor house. Summer pageants and other events are held here. www.carewcastle.com **17 D6**

Carmarthen Castle *Carmarthen/Caerfyrddin, Carmarthenshire* A ruined castle in the form of a Norman fortress, first built in 1109, rebuilt in stone in 1181, and sacked and destroyed several times before being converted into a prison in the 18th century. It retains a 14th-century gatehouse, and part of the medieval drawbridge was excavated in 2003. www.cadw.gov.wales **21 C8**

Carreg Cennen Castle *Trapp, Carmarthenshire* A hilltop castle in mountainous farming terrain, built under Edward I on a site probably occupied by Romans and prehistoric peoples, and including a prehistoric cave. www.cadw.gov.wales **23 D6**

Castell Cilgerran *Cilgerran, Pembrokeshire* A castle dramatically sited at the top of a gorge overlooking the River Teifi, where coracles can sometimes be seen on the river (there are annual coracle races in August). www.nationaltrust.org.uk **30 D3**

Haverfordwest Castle *Haverfordwest/Hwlffordd, Pembrokeshire* The shell of an early 12th-century castle containing an old prison and police station housing the county archives, plus a museum on the history of the castle and the town. **17 A5**

Kidwelly Castle *Kidwelly/Cydweli, Carmarthenshire* A well-preserved half-moon-shaped castle overlooking the Gwendraeth Estuary, originally built in 1106 by Roger, Bishop of Salisbury, to defend the road to west Wales after the Norman conquest, and turned into a stone stronghold under Edward I. It retains its imposing outer walls sheltering inner fortifications with four towers. www.cadw.gov.wales **21 F8**

Llawhaden Castle *Llawhaden, Pembrokeshire* An impressive 12th-century castle overlooking the valley, built to protect the estates of the bishops of St David's and located on the Landsker Line, which divided the Welsh-speaking north from the English-speaking south. www.cadw.gov.wales **17 A7**

Manorbier Castle *Manorbier/Maenorbŷr, Pembrokeshire* A tranquilly located 12th-century castle overlooking a sandy beach, described by Gerald of Wales as 'the pleasantest spot in all Wales's, with an outer bailey with relics from the English Civil War, an imposing Great Gatehouse, and some huge industrial hearths with Flemish chimneys. www.manorbiercastle.co.uk **17 E7**

Pembroke Castle *Front St, Pembroke Dock/Doc Penfro, Pembrokeshire* A 13th-century castle on the banks of the River Cleddau, with a museum, a complete set of walls, one of the finest great keeps in Britain, a brass rubbing centre and a summer programme of reenactments and other events. www.pembroke-castle.co.uk **17 D5**

Picton Castle and Woodland Gardens *The Rhos, near Haverfordwest/Hwlffordd, Pembrokeshire* A 13th-century castle still inhabited by the descendants of the first owner, Sir John Wogan, with splendid 40-acre woodland gardens and an art gallery. www.pictoncastle.co.uk **17 B6**

Tenby Castle *Tenby/Dinbych-y-Pysgod, Pembrokeshire* A ruined castle overlooking the harbour, with the well-preserved town walls it formed William de Valences' defensive plan for Tenby. **17 D8**

Wye Valley and Vale of Usk

Abergavenny Castle *Abergavenny/Fenni, Monmouthshire* A ruined Norman castle overlooking the River Usk, the focus for more than 300 years of border warfare and seat of the medieval lords of Abergavenny. Living history events are held, and the grounds contain Abergavenny Museum (see *Local history*). **26 E4**

Caldicot Castle and Country Park *Church Rd, Caldicot, Monmouthshire* A splendid castle begun by the Normans, completed by the end of the 14th century and restored as a family home in the 19th century, set in 55 acres of attractive wooded parkland and gardens, with audio tours, living-history events, outdoor activities such as orienteering and pond-dipping, hands-on activities, an adventure play area, and a tearoom. www.visitmonmouthshire.com **14 E1**

Chepstow Castle *Chepstow/Cas-Gwent, Monmouthshire* The extensive remains of one of Britain's first stone-built castles, originally built in the 11th century by a supporter of William the Conquerer, then modified and developed throughout the Middle Ages and strengthened during the Civil War. www.cadw.gov.wales **14 D2**

Monmouth Castle *Monmouth/Trefynwy, Monmouthshire* A castle begun c.1068 by the Earl of Hereford, of which only the ruined Great Tower and Hall remain. The small medieval-style herb garden has plants and trees from the era of Henry V, born in the castle, and Great Castle House contains the Royal Monmouthshire Royal Engineers Regimental Museum (see *Military history*). **27 E8**

Newport Castle *Newport/Casnewydd, City and County of Newport* The remains of an early-14th-century fortress built to guard the settlement and control the river crossing; most of the surviving stone structure dates from the following century, when it was strengthened. **13 E6**

Raglan Castle *Raglan/Rhaglan, Monmouthshire* A 1430s medieval fortress-palace built on the site of a small Norman castle, with an unusual hexagonal tower with an elaborate drawbridge and a closet tower housing an exhibition on the history of Raglan. www.cadw.gov.wales **27 F6**

Houses and gardens

Anglesey and Snowdonia

Aberconwy House *Castle Street, Conwy, Conwy* A medieval merchant's house with period rooms and an exhibition about life in the town from Roman times on. www.nationaltrust.org.uk **69 D5**

Llys Euryn *Rhos on Sea, Conwy* A ruined manor house built on the site of the Palace of Ednyfed Fychan, overlooked by the remains of a hillfort. **69 C6**

Plas Mawr *Conwy, Conwy* One of the UK's best-preserved Elizabethan townhouses, with a gatehouse, stepped gables, a lookout tower and an original interior with elaborate plaster ceilings and wooden screens. www.cadw.gov.wales **69 D5**

Plas Newydd *Llanfairpwllgwyngyll, Isle of Anglesey* The 18th-century house of the First Marquess of Anglesey, built in a classical meets mock-Gothic style and boasting a 1930s interior, an exhibition about Whistler and a military museum. www.nationaltrust.org.uk **67 F7**

Plas yn Rhiw *Rhiw, Gwynedd* A small 16th-century Welsh manor house in ornamental grounds, restored in 1938 by the Keating sisters and affording views across Cardigan Bay. www.nationaltrust.org.uk **50 C4**

Ty Mawr Wybrnant *Penmachno, Conwy* The restored 16th- and 17th-century house where Bishop William Morgan, the first translator of the whole Bible into Welsh, lived,

◀ Plas Newydd
Leighton Collins / Dreamstime

ɔw housing a display of Welsh Bibles. www.nationaltrust.org.uk **60 D3**

ɿe Ugly House *Ty Hill, Capel Curig, ɔnwy* A 'Ty Un Nos' or 'house built ɿernight' (under ancient law anyone ho built a house between sunset and ɿnrise could claim the freehold), now e Snowdonia Society HQ with an ɿhibition about its work. **60 C2**

ɿern Isaf *Penmaen Park, ɿnfairfechan, Conwy* A 1900 ɿts and Crafts house with original rniture and William Morris fabrics. **8 D3**

orth East Wales

ɿrddig House *near Wrexham / ɿrecsam, Wrexham* An 1680s house ɿith 18th- and 19th-century furniture, ɿpressive outbuildings (including a undry, bakehouse and smithy) and ɿ 18th-century walled garden with a ɿctorian parterre, yew walk and the ɿational Collection of Ivies. ɿwww.nationaltrust.org.uk **63 E7**

ɿas Newydd *near Llangollen, ɿenbighshire* A black-and-white ɿmbered house that belonged to the ɿcentric Irish 'Ladies of Llangollen', ɿho dressed as men and entertained ɿe likes of Sir Walter Scott and William ɿordsworth here. The beautiful ɿounds are now a public park. **62 F5**

ɿwansea, Gower and Vale ɿf Neath

ɿxwich Castle *Oxwich, Swansea* The ɿmains of a splendid mock-fortified ɿdor mansion on a headland above ɿxwich Bay, probably built on the site ɿ an earlier stronghold (hence the ɿame). www.cadw.gov.wales **8 E4**

ɿalleys of South Wales

ɿyfarthfa Castle and Park *Brecon ɿd, Merthyr Tydfil / Merthyr Tudful, ɿerthyr Tydfil* A mock-Gothic mansion ɿuilt in 1824 for William Crawshay , who set up the town's original ɿonworks, now housing a museum ɿn local history and the industrial ɿevolution, an art gallery with works ɿy Augustus John, Vanessa Bell and ɿthers, Victorian tearooms and 160 ɿcres of attractive parkland. **23 F5**

ɿlancaiach Fawr Manor *Nelson, ɿeharris, Merthyr Tydfil* A 1645 manor ɿouse hosting reenactments of the ɿveryday life of the owner, Colonel ɿrichard, and his servants more than ɿ50 years ago and the effect of the ɿivil War on the household. **12 C2**

ɿest Wales

ɿlanerchaeron Mansion *Tregaron, ɿeredigion* A National Trust owned ɿansion house designed by John Nash ɿ the 1790s and newly open to the ɿublic after extensive restoration, with ɿarm buildings and gardens. There ɿre various walks around the estate, ɿhrough the churchyard, and around ɿe home farm, Wig Wen. ɿwww.nationaltrust.org.uk **32 A2**

ɿewton House *Dinefwr Park, ɿlandeilo, Carmarthenshire* A 1660 ɿouse with a Victorian-Gothic ɿacade, surrounded by 18th-century ɿndscaped parkland containing a ɿedieval deer park with fallow deer and ɿinefwr White Park cattle, a fountain garden and a boardwalk. There is an exhibition on the role of Dinefwr in Welsh history, guided tours of the house and deer park, and access to Dinefwr Castle. www.nationaltrust.org.uk **23 C5**

Scolton Manor House and Country Park *Spittal, Pembrokeshire* A Victorian manor house with displays of historical artefacts, a steam train, a smithy and wheelwright's shop, surrounded by an eco-friendly country park and woodland. www.visitpembrokeshire.com **19 E7**

Tudor Merchants House *Quay Hill, Tenby / Dinbych-y-Pysgod, Pembrokeshire* A narrow three-storey house that belonged to a wealthy merchant in Tudor times, owned by the National Trust and giving an insight into Tudor times. www.nationaltrust.org.uk **17 D8**

Wye Valley and Vale of Usk

Tredegar House *Tredegar Park, Newport / Casnewydd, City and County of Newport* A fine 17th-century Charles II mansion with guided tours taking in the imposing staterooms and the servants' quarters. The surrounding 90-acre park has a playground, a woodland walk, a jogging trail and a boating lake. **13 E5**

Roman sites

Anglesey and Snowdonia

Canovium Roman Settlement *Caerhun, Gwynedd* A archaeological site with the remains of two prehistoric forts, a Roman fort, a Roman road, a chambered tomb, and Iron Age and medieval farms and field systems. **69 E5**

Monuments and ancient sites

Anglesey and Snowdonia

Barclodiad-y-Gawres *near Aberffraw, Isle of Anglesey* A chambered tomb spectacularly sited overlooking a bay, containing five carved stones. **66 E3**

Bryn Celli Ddu *Llanddaniel Fab, Isle of Anglesey* A late Neolithic tomb built on a previous circle henge, with a 27ft passage leading to the burial chamber. **67 E7**

Din Lligwy *near Ty-Mawr, Isle of Anglesey* A 4th-century settlement surrounded by a low stone wall, within which are the remains of nine huts, two of them circular. Nearby are the remains of Capel Lligwy, a 12th-century chapel. **67 B6**

Hendre Waelod *Llansanffraid Glan Conwy, Conwy* A Neolithic burial chamber on the bank of the River Conwy, a rare portal dolmen with traditional high portal stones. **69 E5**

Lligwy Burial Chamber *near Ty-Mawr, Isle of Anglesey* A 28-ton capstone covering a burial chamber believed to have been used in the Neolithic period and the Bronze Age. **67 B7**

Maen y Bardd (Stone of the Bard) *Rowen, Conwy* A Neolithic burial chamber above the River Conwy, thought to date back to 3500BC, with sidestones and capstones that project to form a portal area. **60 A3**

Ty Mawr Hut Circles *Holyhead / Caergybi, Isle of Anglesey* A small late Neolithic or early Bronze Age agricultural settlement comprised of about 19 structures spread over 15–20 acres of mountainside. **66 C1**

Ty Newydd *near Llanfaelog, Isle of Anglesey* A restored cromlech that is all that remains of a Neolithic tomb that remained in use into the Bronze Age. **66 E3**

Cardiff and Vale of Glamorgan

Tinkinswood Burial Chamber *near St Nicholas, Vale of Glamorgan* A Neolithic burial chamber believed to have the biggest capstone in the country, at about 40 tonnes, and originally containing broken human bones from 40 people. **4 B1**

Valleys of South Wales

Cefn Golau Cholera Cemetery *Tredegar, Blaenau Gwent* A mountainside cemetery where at least 200 local cholera victims were buried in the mid 19th century, with standing and fragmented gravestones. **25 F7**

West Wales

Carew Cross *Carew, Pembrokeshire* An early-Christian intricately carved Celtic stone cross, constructed as a memorial to Mareddud ap Edwin, joint ruler of the kingdom of Deheubarth (south-west Wales) in 1035. **17 D6**

Carn Ingli *Newport / Trefdraeth, Pembrokeshire* The remains of a large hillfort with breathtaking views over the hills, vales and coast, together with prehistoric hut circles and stones. **19 B9**

Carreg Samson *Abercastle, Pembrokeshire* A fine example of a cromlech (exposed Neolithic burial chamber). **18 C5**

Castell Henllys *near Eglwyswrw, Pembrokeshire* A reconstructed Iron Age hillfort, with ancient animal breeds and displays by traditional craftspeople. **30 E2**

Merlin's Hill *Alltyfyrddin Farm, Abergwili, Carmarthenshire* An Iron Age fort on a hill where, according to legend, Merlin is imprisoned, accessed via guided walks over ancient pathways. The farm on which it is located has a heritage centre dedicated to local history and agriculture, milking displays, meet-the-animals sessions, a play area and a picnic site. **22 C1**

Pentre Ifan Burial Chamber *near Newport / Trefdraeth, Pembrokeshire* A fine cromlech with an intact 15-tonne capstone, set in the heart of the Preseli Hills (see *Other natural features*), source of the 'spotted dolerite' in the inner sanctum of Stonehenge. **19 B9**

Wye Valley and Vale of Usk

Fortress Baths *Caerleon / Caerllion, City and County of Newport* The remains of the 'leisure centre' of an important base for Roman legionary troops, founded in AD75, which had a gym, baths and swimming pool. Nearby are the remains of an amphitheatre and barracks. **13 D6**

▲ **Pentre Ifan** Helen Hotson / Dreamstime

Religious buildings

Anglesey and Snowdonia

Gwydir Uchaf Chapel *Llanrwst, Conwy* A 17th-century family chapel in the woods above Llanrwst, famous for its painted ceiling. By arrangement only. **60 B4**

Llanaber and St Bodfan Church *Barmouth / Abermaw, Gwynedd* A 13th-century church housing the late 5th- or early 6th-century Llanaber stones and boasting a south doorway held to be one of the country's best examples of Early English architecture. **52 E4**

Llanbadrig Church *Cemaes, Isle of Anglesey* The 'Church of Saint Patrick', built on a site of religious worship dating back to 440AD, with Islamic influences (stipulated by Muslim benefactor Lord Stanley of Alderly). **66 A4**

Llandrillo-yn-Rhos Church *Llandrillo-yn-Rhos, Conwy* A church with 13th-century pointed arches representing an early structure believed to have been the private chapel of Ednyfed Fychan Seneschal, and a 'Rector's Chair' built to hold flares in case enemy ships were sighted. **69 C6**

Llangelynin Old Church *Llanaelhaearn, Gwynedd* A church with a 15th-century chancel and 16th-century north chapel, south porch and east window. The churchyard contains the Holy Well of St Celynin, said to cure sick children, and the footings of an ancient inn for mountain travellers. **58 F3**

St Cwyfan Church *near Aberffraw, Isle of Anglesey* A seabound, largely Victorian church with 7th-century origins, cut off from the mainland by erosion but still holding services in summer. **66 F4**

St Mary's Church *Caerhun, Gwynedd* An ancient church built mostly of Roman stone blocks or 'ashlars' imported from Chester, built on the site of Kanovium Roman fort. Above the church door and the south chapel are three medieval carvings. **67 F8**

St Trillo's Chapel *Rhos on Sea, Conwy* A tiny 6th-century chapel built over a holy well, used as a place of special prayer. Visits by arrangement. **69 C6**

St Tudno's Church *Great Orme, Llandudno, Conwy* A 12th-century church on the site where the 6th-century Celtic monk Tudno founded his cell in a small cave on the headland (still visible but difficult to get to), holding open-air services overlooking the sea. **69 C5**

Cardiff and Vale of Glamorgan

Ewenny Priory *near Bridgend / Pen-y-Bont ar Ogwr, Bridgend* The restored ruins of a strongly fortified priory founded in the mid 12th century as a cell of the Benedictine abbey of Gloucester, with impressive walls and gates, remodelled c.1300. The nave still serves as the parish church. **3 A5**

Llandaff Cathedral *Cathedral Green, Llandaff, Cardiff* A cathedral on the site of a religious community founded c.AD560 by St Teilo, dedicated to the Celtic saints Dyfrig and Illtyd, and comprising every style of medieval architecture. Heavily restored in 1882 and after WWII, it contains a striking aluminium sculpture by Jacob Epstein. www.llandaffcathedral.org.uk **4 A3**

St Illtud's Church *Llantwit Major / Llanilltud Fawr, Vale of Glamorgan* A medieval church on the site of a church and religious school founded by St Illtud c.AD500, with a collection of Celtic crosses. **3 C6**

Mid Wales and Brecon Beacons

Brecon Cathedral *Brecon / Aberhonddu, Powys* A cathedral with its origins in a Benedictine priory set up on the site at the end of the 12th century, retaining some Norman elements, though it was expanded in the 13th century and altered and added to in the 14th century. In the 1860s it underwent large-scale restoration under Sir Gilbert Scott. There is a Heritage Centre and exhibition space. **25 B5**

Pennant Melangell Church *Pennant-Melangell, Powys* A remodelled 12th-century church added onto a medieval shrine to Irish princess Melangell, who lived a life of contemplation here; the excavated and restored shrine is a place of pilgrimage again. The church contains two stone effigies, a medieval font, and a 15th-century rood screen depicting the story of Melangell, as well as the Green Man, the woodland spirit of Celtic myth. **55 C5**

St Nicholas *Montgomery / Trefaldwyn, Powys* A 12th-century church with

▼ **St Cwyfan Church** Gail Johnson / Dreamstime

later alterations, containing important wooden carvings, some brought from nearby Chirbury Priory. **47 D8**

North East Wales

Leicester's Church *Denbigh / Dinbych, Denbighshire* The remains of the only large new church built during the reign of Elizabeth I, begun by Robert Dudley, Earl of Leicester, in 1578. **62 A1**

Llangar Church *Corwen, Denbighshire* A white-painted medieval church with early-Georgian furnishings and some restored 15th-century wall paintings. **62 F2**

Rug Chapel *Corwen, Denbighshire* A rare little-altered 17th-century private chapel, with an elaborately carved and painted ceiling, a chandelier decorated with cherubs, and a painted gallery. **62 F2**

St Asaph Cathedral *St Asaph / Llanelwy, Denbighshire* Britain's smallest cathedral, founded on a site of worship dating back to AD560 and restored by Sir George Gilbert Scott in 1870. In the grounds are a monument to the first Welsh translations of the Book of Common Prayer and Bible by a local lawyer and bishop. ▣www.cadw.gov.wales **70 E2**

St Deiniol's Church *Hawarden / Penarlâg, Flintshire* A large church recorded in the Domesday Book, with a 14th-century nave, aisles and chancel arch, restored by Sir George Gilbert Scott after a fire in the 19th century. The Whitley Chapel has some fine 17th- and 18th-century monuments. **63 A7**

St Giles' Church *Temple Row, Wrexham / Wrecsam, Wrexham* A late 15th- and early 16th-century church with a Perpendicular tower dubbed one of the 'seven wonders of Wales's and on which the tower of the Houses of Parliament is said to have been modelled. **63 D7**

St Mary's Church *Bodelwyddan, Denbighshire* A landmark church erected by Lady Willoughby de Broke in memory of her husband in 1856–60, known as the 'Marble Church' because of the 13 types of marble inside. It contains some of the finest Victorian wood carving in Britain. **70 D2**

St Winefride's Well *Greenfield Valley Heritage and Country Park Holywell / Treffynon, Flintshire* The only shrine in Britain with an unbroken history of pilgrimage, at the spot where a local chieftain is said to have beheaded Winefride after she spurned his advances in AD660. A chapel above the well has a camberbeam roof and carved corbels. **71 D5**

Valle Crucis Abbey *near Llangollen, Denbighshire* The Gothic stone ruins of a 13th-century Cistercian abbey founded by a Welsh prince, with an almost-intact chapterhouse. **62 F5**

Swansea, Gower and Vale of Neath

Llangyfelach Church *Llangyfelach, Swansea* One of only three churches in Wales with a detached tower. The grounds were once the site of a monastery founded by St David, one of the earliest Christian worship sites in Wales, and inside are three pre-Norman carved stones. **9 C7**

Margam Abbey Church and Stones Museum *near Port Talbot, Neath Port Talbot* The only Cistercian foundation in Wales with an intact nave, founded in 1147. Other remains include a 12-sided chapterhouse in the early English style, and there is a small museum with inscribed pre-Romanesque, Roman and Celtic stones and crosses, some found within the Margam area. **10 E2**

Neath Abbey *Neath / Castell-nedd, Neath Port Talbot* A ruined abbey in a tranquil setting on the banks of the Tennant Canal, founded by Norman baron Richard de Granville in 1130 and described as the 'fairest abbey in all Wales's by Tudor historian John Leland. ▣www.cadw.gov.wales **10 C2**

Valleys of South Wales

St Illtyd's *Brynithel, Blaenau Gwent* A restored deconsecrated 12th-century church with many original features, a roughly circular pre-Norman churchyard and a Norman motte that may have been built over a prehistoric barrow or cairn. **12 B4**

Vaynor Church *Vaynor, Merthyr Tydfil* An 1870 church on a 9th-century site of worship, with a castellated tower remaining from the first stone church of 1295. On the steeple end is an inscription commemorating Catherine Morgan, who lived under the reign of seven monarchs (1688–1794). **25 E5**

West Wales

Abaty St Dogmaels *St Dogmaels / Llandudoch, Pembrokeshire* A 12th-century abbey founded by Benedictine monks on the site of an earlier Celtic monastery. The adjoining church of St Thomas the Martyr contains the Sagranus Stone, the markings and Latin inscription on which helped in the deciphering of the ancient Goidelic language. **30 C3**

Abaty Ystrad Fflur *Pontrhydfendigaid, Ceredigion* The Cistercian abbey of Strata Florida ('Vale of Flowers'), founded in 1164 and retaining a superb Norman arch. Once the 'Westminster of Wales', it was the burial place of some of the last Welsh princes and princesses. **39 E7**

Caldey Abbey *Caldey Island, Tenby / Dinbych-y-Pysgod, Pembrokeshire* The home of Cistercian monks, who farm the tiny island on which it lies and produce famous perfume and chocolate. There is also a medieval priory, a lighthouse, a museum, a tea garden, a sandy beach and splendid views. **17 D8**

Church of the Holy Cross *Llanerchaeron, Ciliau Aeron, Ceredigion* A tiny church built c.1400 on the site of a much earlier Celtic church that was a strategic point on the pilgrim route to Bardsey Island, where 20,000 Celtic saints are said to be buried. Set on a National Trust headland, it overlooks secluded Traeth Mwnt beach and has glorious views. **32 A3**

Ciffig Church *Whitland / Hendy-Gwyn, Carmarthenshire* A listed 12th-century church with a preaching window by the pulpit. **20 D3**

Eglwys St Padarn Church *Llanbadarn Fawr, Ceredigion* The church where, according to legend, St Padarn and his associate Cadfan founded a religious order after sailing from Brittany with 847 monks in the 6th century. It has an early chapel, a cell where St Padarn is said to have lived, and an exhibition on scholarship at Llanbadarn within the context of Welsh history. **38 B5**

Lamphey Bishops Palace *Lamphey, Pembrokeshire* The extensive, renovated remains of the grand medieval palace built for the bishops of St David's in the 13th century. Special events are held in summer. ▣www.cadw.gov.wales **17 D6**

Mathry Church *Mathry, Pembrokeshire* An 1869 church built on ancient foundations with a circular churchyard that may have been occupied by an Iron Age settlement, containing two early Christian sculptured stones. **19 C5**

National Shrine of Our Lady of Cardigan *Aberystwyth Rd, Cardigan / Aberteifi, Ceredigion* The national shrine of the Roman Catholic Church in Wales; according to legend, the original statue (believed destroyed under Henry VIII) kept returning to the bank of the Teifi where it had first been discovered, until a church was built there to house it. **30 C3**

St Brynach *Nevern, Pembrokeshire* A church in an ancient hamlet, with the Latin- and Ogam-inscribed Vitalianus Stone by the porch, and a 13th-century wheel-headed Celtic cross in the churchyard, next to a yew tree famous for 'bleeding' red sap. It is overlooked by a ravine topped by Nevern Castle, a motte-and-bailey earthwork. **30 D1**

St David's Bishops Palace *St David's / Tyddewi, Pembrokeshire* A ruined 14th-century palace built by Bishop de Gower. It retains its grand battlements, curtain walls, gatehouse and entrance to the Great Hall. ▣www.cadw.gov.wales **18 D3**

St David's Cathedral *St David's / Tyddewi, Pembrokeshire* A magnificent ancient church built in the 'Vale of the Roses' to conceal it from Viking raiders, on the site of the 6th-century St David's monastery, and restored by Sir George Gilbert Scott in 1862–77. It is still used as a place of worship and concert venue, and guided tours are available. ▣www.stdavidscathedral.org.uk **18 D3**

St David's Church *Llanddewi Brefi, near Tregaron, Ceredigion* A church built on the site of a college founded in 1187 by the Bishop of St David's, with some ancient monuments (partly destroyed during rebuilding in the 1800s) and a statue of St David (said to have performed a miracle here). **39 F6**

St Edgwad Church *Llanegwad, Carmarthenshire* A church on the site of several monasteries and religious cells, begun in the 10th or 11th century and restored in the 19th century. **22 C3**

St Govan's Chapel and Well *near Bosherston, Pembrokeshire* A tiny 13th-century hermit's single-chamber cell built into the cliffs of St Govan's head, accessible via 52 rough stone steps. Below is a dry well, the waters of which were famous for their healing powers. **17 F5**

St Llawddog *Cenarth, Ceredigion* An 1872 church that replaced an earlier ruined church, with a font bowl dating back at least as far as the 12th century, once used as a trough, and an inscribed 'sarsen' stone of millstone grit in the churchyard. **31 D5**

St Martin *Laugharne / Talacharn, Carmarthenshire* The Norman church where Dylan Thomas and his wife Caitlin are buried, restored in the 15th century and in 1873, with a Celtic cross-slab, a painted nave ceiling, and a 15th-century Italian brocade cope (not on display). **21 E6**

St Nons *St David's / Tyddewi, Pembrokeshire* A holy well, retreat and shrine dedicated to the mother of St David. **18 D3**

St Peter *Carmarthen / Caerfyrddin, Carmarthenshire* A large church with a tower, said to be on the site of a Celtic pre-Norman church. Parts of the church date to the 13th century, and it has a bishop's court and several 17th- to 19th-century memorials to well-known local figures. **21 C8**

Soar y Mynydd Mountain Chapel *near Tregaron, Ceredigion* Wales's remotest chapel, built in 1882 with an attached house and stable for visiting preachers, and still in use. **39 F6**

Wye Valley and Vale of Usk

Llanthony Priory *Llanthony, Monmouth-shire* A ruined medieval Augustinian priory in the Brecon Beacons National Park (see *National Parks and AONBs*), built on the site of a hermit's cell and dissolved in 1536. **26 B3**

St Woolos Cathedral *Newport / Casnewydd, City and County of Newport* Built on an early 6th-century site of worship, the building is a 12th-century Norman church within a later mediaeval structure, restored in Victorian times and designated a cathedral in 1929. **13 E6**

Tintern Abbey *Tintern Parva, Monmouthshire* An imposing and well-preserved Cistercian abbey founded on the banks of the Wye in 1131, the inspiration for a poem by Wordsworth. ▣www.cadw.gov.wales **14 B2**

Museums and galleries

Art and crafts

See also Picton Castle and Woodland Gardens; St Donats Castle (both *Castles*); Cyfarthfa Castle and Park (*Houses and gardens*); Amgueddfa Ceredigion Aberystwyth; Brecknock Museum and Art Gallery; Goytre Wharf Heritage, Activity and Study Centre; Neath Museum and Art Gallery; Newport Museum and Art Gallery; Parc Howard Museum and Art Gallery; Tenby Museum and Art Gallery (all *Local History*); Porthcawl Museum (*Military History*).

Anglesey and Snowdonia

Oriel Mostyn Gallery *12 Heol Vaughan, Llandudno, Conwy* An adventurous contemporary art gallery with exhibitions by major international artists. ▣www.mostyn.org **69 C5**

Plas Glyn y Weddw Art Gallery *Pwllheli, Gwynedd* One of Wales's oldest art galleries, set in a Victorian-Gothic mansion with landscaped gardens and displaying mainly Welsh work, plus Swansea and Nangarw porcelain. ▣www.oriel.org.uk **51 A7**

Royal Cambrian Academy *Crown Lane, Conwy, Conwy* Wales's most prestigious art institution, showing work from Wales and the rest of Britain. ▣https://rcaconwy.org **69 D5**

Cardiff and Vale of Glamorgan

Chapter *Market Rd, Canton, Cardiff / Caerdydd, Cardiff* Wales's contemporary arts flagship, with exhibitions, performance and films from Wales and around the world. The main space has three theatres, two cinemas, a gallery, more than 60 cultural workspaces, bars and a café. ▣www.chapter.org **4 A3**

◄ **The Norwegian Church, Cardiff Bay** Whitcomberd / Dreamstime

ed Hills Rural Artspace
Hilary, near Cowbridge/Y Bont Faen, le of Glamorgan Landscape-based works on a 180-acre former farm th studios, exhibition and workshop aces in former outbuildings and rns, a sculpture trail and an organic é. **3 A6**

tional Museum Cardiff / ngueddfa Genedlaethol erdydd *Cathays Park, rdiff/Caerdydd, Cardiff* A world-ss museum and gallery with e world's biggest collection of pressionist art outside France, plus tural history and science displays. ıttps://museum.wales/cardiff **A3**

rwegian Church Arts Centre *rbour Drive, Cardiff/Caerdydd, rdiff* A former church built for lors, dockers and their families, th an art gallery, concert hall and fé. It was here that Roald Dahl was ristened. **4 A3**

rner House Art Gallery *Plymouth , Penarth, Vale of Glamorgan* mporary exhibitions of paintings m the collection of the National useums and Galleries of Wales, plus a new space for contemporary photography.
https://turnerhouse.wales **4 B3**

Mid Wales and Brecon Beacons

Lake Vyrnwy Sculpture Trail *Brynawel, Llanwddyn, Powys* A growing trail begun by local artist Andy Hancock in 1997, with outsize wildlife sculptures in timber and stone, including otters, badgers and bluebells, plus carved benches, wall hangings, storytelling seats, willow lanterns and mazes. **54 E5**

North East Wales

Ruthin Craft Centre Gallery *Park Road, Ruthin/Rhuthun, Denbighshire* An applied arts centre displaying contemporary pieces from around Britain. www.ruthincraftcentre.org.uk **62 C3**

Tŷ Pawb *Rhosddu Road, Wrexham/Wrecsam, Wrexham* Contemporary visual arts and crafts exhibitions by artists from Wales and farther afield.
www.typawb.wales **63 D7**

Swansea, Gower and Vale of Neath

Glynn Vivian Art Gallery *Alexandra Rd, Swansea/Abertawe, Swansea* Internationally renowned collections of Swansea and Nantgarw pottery and porcelain, other British, European and oriental wares, and a collection of 20th-century fine art by Welsh and Welsh-based artists, such as Augustus and Gwen John, and other British and European artists (including Gustave Dore and Barbara Epstein), plus a contemporary art programme. **9 D8**

► **Ffestiniog Railway** Serjio74 / Dreamstime

Valleys of South Wales

Llantarnam Grange Arts Centre *St David's Rd, Cwmbran/Cwmbrân, Torfaen* An arts and crafts centre with regularly changing exhibitions and workshops. **13 C5**

Model House *Llantrisant, Rhondda Cynon Taff* An award-winning contemporary craft and design centre in a converted Victorian building, with exhibitions, demonstrations, workshops, talks and seminars, and 10 craft studios where visitors can see work in production. There is also an exhibition on the history of coin production (Llantrisant has been home to the Royal Mint since the 1960s).
www.llantrisantgallery.com **11 F7**

West Wales

Canolfan Y Celfyddydau Aberystwyth Arts Centre *University campus, Penglais, Aberystwyth, Ceredigion* Wales's largest arts centre, containing contemporary art galleries hosting painting, sculpture, photography, ceramics (of which there is a permanent gallery) and other craft exhibitions (free).
www.aberystwythartscentre.co.uk **38 B4**

Oriel Q Gallery *High St, Narberth/Arberth, Pembrokeshire* Contemporary work by local artists, both new and established. **20 E2**

Waterfront Gallery *Sail Loft, The Docks, Milford Haven/ Aberdaugleddau, Pembrokeshire* A local arts and crafts showcase.
https://thewaterfrontgallery.co.uk **16 C4**

Science and technology

Anglesey and Snowdonia

Ffestiniog Power Station Hydro Centre Tours and Stwlan Dam *Tanygrisiau, Gwynedd* Tours of Britain's first pump-storage hydroelectric power station, followed by a trip up to Stwlan dam reservoir with its panoramic views. www.fhc.co.uk/en/power-stations/ffestiniog-power-station/ **60 F1**

Cardiff and Vale of Glamorgan

Cardiff Bay Barrage *Penarth, Vale of Glamorgan* One of Europe's most advanced engineering projects, key to the city's docklands regeneration, viewable by guided tour.
www.cardiffharbour.com **4 B3**

Techniquest *Stuart St, Cardiff/ Caerdydd, Cardiff* A science-discovery centre with more than 160 interactive displays, a laboratory and a hi-tech Science Theatre.
www.techniquest.org **4 A3**

Mid Wales and Brecon Beacons

Centre for Alternative Technology *Machynlleth, Powys* An award-winning centre with Europe's largest ecological exhibition, including working examples of wind, water and solar power, energy conservation, environmentally sound buildings and organic growing.
www.cat.org.uk **45 C6**

Spaceguard UK *Llanshay Lane, Knighton/Tref-y-Clawdd, Powys* A centre for studies into the threat posed to the Earth by collisions with asteroids and comets, with telescopes, Europe's largest camera obscura, a small planetarium and a weather station.
https://spaceguardcentre.com **42 D3**

Swansea, Gower and Vale of Neath

Environment Centre *Pier St, Swansea/Abertawe, Swansea* An environmental information, education, research and activity centre, with year-round exhibitions and a Fairtrade coffeeshop.
www.environmentcentre.org.uk **9 D8**

West Wales

Internal Fire *Castell Pridd Farm, Tan-y-groes, Ceredigion* A museum tracing the history of the internal combustion engine
www.internalfire.com **31 C5**

Rheidol Hydro-electric Power Station *Cwm Rheidol, Capel Bangor, Ceredigion* A power station in the lovely Rheidol Valley, offering free guided tours. It has a nearby Visitor Centre, with audio-visual exhibitions, and nature trails. **39 C7**

Family attractions

ee also *Country, coastal and forest parks; nimal attractions; Beaches and resorts.*

nglesey and Snowdonia

nglesey Model Village *between Dwyran and ewboroughIsle of Anglesey* A scale model village eaturing many of Anglesey's landmarks, in an acre f landscaped gardens with water features. **58 A4**

oel Farm Park *Brynsiencyn, Anglesey/Ynys Môn* scenic farm park overlooking Caernarfon Castle nd the Menai Strait. It offers tractor, trailer and ony rides, and opportunities to feed the animals. here is also a country café and artisan chocolate op on-site. www.foelfarm.co.uk **58 A5**

arlequin Puppet Theatre *Rhos on Sea, Conwy* ritain's oldest permanent puppet theatre, set up in 958. www.puppetmagic.co.uk **69 C6**

landudno Pier *Llandudno, Conwy* A recreational ier in an Indian-Gothic style with iron lacework, uilt in 1878 and the longest in Wales. **69 C5**

ictoria Pier *Colwyn Bay/Bae Colwyn, Conwy* A ictorian pier with a variety of amusements. **69 D7**

ardiff and Vale of Glamorgan

arry Island Pleasure Park *Barry Island, ale of Glamorgan* A summer venue with more han 50 rides, including a log flume and gentle des for small children.
www.barryislandpleasurepark.wales **4 C2**

Mid Wales and Brecon Beacons

antref Adventure Farm *Near Llanfrynach, recon/Aberhonddu, Powys* An award-winning arm with outdoor play areas, a swamp ride and urope's longest sledge ride. There are animal hows, including bottle-feeding lambs, ig-racing, and pony rides, among others.
www.cantref.com **25 B6**

orth East Wales

reenacres Animal Park *Queensferry, Flintshire/ ıry Fflint* A park with alpacas, llamas, donkeys, ybrid wolves, rabbits, ducks, among others. isitors can enjoy amusement and fun fair rides, tractor tours, pony rides and magic shows throughout the year. www.greenacresanimalpark.co.uk **71 F8**

SC2 Rhyl West Parade, *Rhyl/Y Rhyl, Denbighshire/ Sir Ddinbych* A centre for both outdoor and indoor play, including a water park, Ninja TAG assault course and adventure playground.
https://sc2rhyl.co.uk **70 C2**

Xplore! *Henblas Street, Wrexham/Wrecsam* A science discovery centre, with hands-on exhibitions illuminating a wide range of topics from earthquakes to space travel and surgery.
https://xplorescience.co.uk **63 D7**

Swansea, Gower and Vale of Neath

Aquadome *Afan Lido, Aberavon, Neath Port Talbot* A theme pool with a giant spaceship, an Inca temple, a lily pond, bubble loungers, river rides and more.**10 D2**

Black Pill Lido and Adventure Playground *Black Pill, Swansea* An innovative activity area for children of all ages and abilities, including a whale-shaped paddling pool with interactive elements, two sound sculptures of musical ospreys in the play area, a picnic area and views over Swansea Bay and Mumbles. **9 D7**

LC Waterpark *Oystermouth Road, Swansea/ Abertawe* The country's biggest indoor waterpark, filled with pools, slides, rides and dedicated areas for smaller swimmers. There is a four-storey aquatic themed interactive play area, a café, and a 30-foot indoor climbing wall, for new and experienced climbers. www.thelcswansea.com **9 D8**

Valleys of South Wales

Meadows Farm Village *Gypsy Lane, Caerphilly/ Caerffili* An interactive animal experience, including a variety of species, from meerkats to guinea pigs, wallabies and more. The facility offers a coffee shop and petting areas, with upgraded walkways to ensure easy accessibility for visitors with wheelchairs.
https://themeadowsfarmvillage.co.uk **12 E3**

National Lido of Wales *Ynysangharad War Memorial Park, Pontypridd, Rhondda Cynon Taff/ Rhondda Cynon Taf* Lido Ponty, a restored outdoor pool attraction that often hosts inflatable obstacle course sessions. There is also a children's play area and café. www.rctcbc.gov.uk **11 D8**

Zip World *Hirwaun, Aberdare, Rhondda Cynon Taff/ Rhondda Cynon Taf* An adventure park, home to Phoenix, the fastest seated zip wire in the world, as well as a three-story aerial activity course, a two-seated roller coaster, a bistro and bar. www.zipworld.co.uk **11 A5**

West Wales

Clerkenhill Farm Adventure Walk *Slebech, near Haverfordwest/Hwlffordd, Pembrokeshire* A family farm offering a walk through working farmland, with information boards, adventure activities and quizzes, plus a play area and farm memorabilia. **17 B6**

Dinosaur Park *Gumfreston, near Tenby/Dinbych-y-Pysgod, Pembrokeshire* A dinosaur theme park with indoor and outdoor attractions, including an adventure playground, an activity centre and a woodland trail, plus a daily programme of activities.
www.thedinosaurpark.co.uk **17 D8**

Heatherton World of Activities *St Florence, Tenby/Dinbych-y-Pysgod, Pembrokeshire/Sir Benfro* An award-winning activity centre near Tenby, boasting over 30 adrenaline-fuelled activities, a play zone for children and a golf and bowls zone. This is a dog-friendly attraction, with its own dog agility course.
www.heatherton.co.uk **17 D7**

Oakwood Leisure *Canaston Bridge, Pembrokeshire* A theme park with more than 40 rides and attractions, including Megaphobia, a wooden roller coaster, and many smaller rides for younger children.
www.oakwoodthemepark.co.uk **17 B7**

Transport

See also *Boat Trips.*

Anglesey and Snowdonia

Conwy Suspension Bridge *Conwy, Conwy* An 1826 Thomas Telford designed bridge, now a National Trust property.
www.nationaltrust.org.uk **69 D5**

Ffestiniog Railway *Harbour Station, Porthmadog, Gwynedd* The world's oldest independent railway company, built to carry slate from Blaenau Ffestiniog, now crossing the spectacular scenery of the Snowdonia National Park. There is a sister railway, the Welsh Highland, between Caernarfon and Waunfawr.
www.festrail.co.uk **52 A3**

Great Orme Tramway *Llandudno, Conwy* The only surviving cable-hauled public road tramway still using the original Victorian carriages, providing access to Great Orme Country Park. The Halfway Station has a new tramway exhibition. www.greatormetramway.co.uk **69 C5**

Llanberis Lake Railway *Llanberis, Gwynedd* Forty-minute trips through the spectacular scenery of Padarn Country Park, with views of Snowdon and other mountains.
www.lake-railway.co.uk **59 B7**

Snowdon Mountain Railway
Llanberis, Gwynedd The UK's only public rack and pinion mountain railway, dating back to 1896 and offering spectacular views on its journey from Llanberis to the summit of Snowdon. Open mid March to mid November.
🖳 www.snowdonrailway.co.uk **59 B7**

Talyllyn Railway *Wharf Station, Tywyn, Gwynedd* Two-and-a-half-hour trips by coal-fired narrow-gauge steam train through Snowdonia National Park, with stops for forest walks and a picnic beside a waterfall.
🖳 www.talyllyn.co.uk **44 C2**

Heath Park Miniature Railway and Tramway *King George V Drive East, Heath, Cardiff* Miniature steam, diesel and electric train rides, plus tram rides, through parkland. **4 A3**

Mid Wales and Brecon Beacons
Brecon and Monmouthshire Canal *Brecon / Aberhonddu, Powys* A scenic c.50 km canal through the Brecon Beacons National Park (see *National Parks and AONBs*), built in 1797–1812 and restored by the British Waterways Board. Activities include boat trips, canoeing, fishing, towpath walks (including a section of the Taff Trail; see *Walking, riding and cycling trails*), and it is a good spot to see breeding kingfishers.
🖳 www.breconbeacons.org **25 B5**

National Cycle Collection *Automobile Palace, Temple St, Llandrindod Wells / Llandrindod, Powys* A museum tracing the history of bicycles, with models dating as far back as 1819, old photographs, posters and enamel signs, videos, and displays on racing stars.
🖳 www.cyclemuseum.org.uk **41 F6**

North East Wales
Llangollen Motor Museum *Pentre Felin, Llangollen, Denbighshire* More than 60 vehicles, from cars to invalid carriages, a re-created 1950s village garage, and a small exhibition about the local canal network. **62 F5**

Llangollen Railway *Llangollen, Denbighshire* A restored line with mainly steam-hauled trains running through 12km of stunning Dee Valley scenery, weekends in winter, daily June-Oct.
🖳 www.llangollen-railway.co.uk **62 F5**

Pontcysyllte Aqueduct *Wrexham / Wrecsam, Wrexham* A revolutionary 1795 Thomas Telford aqueduct, now on the list of possible future UNESCO World Heritage sites. Boat trips along the Llangollen Canal and across the aqueduct are available at Chirk Marina. **63 F6**

Swansea, Gower and Vale of Neath
Heart of Wales Line A 180-km route on the national rail network through the dramatic landscapes of rural mid-Wales between Swansea and Shewsbury. 🖳 https://tfw.wales **9 D8**

Neath Canal *Neath / Castell-nedd, Neath Port Talbot* Boat trips along a restored section of the canal north of Resolven, through the magnificent Upper Neath Valley to Aberpergwm. The canal towpath can also be followed by foot as far as Aberdulais. **10 C2**

Valleys of South Wales
Brecon Mountain Railway *Pant, Merthyr Tydfil* Vintage steam locomotive trips into the Brecon Beacons / Bannau Brycheiniog National Park (see *National Parks and AONBs*), along Taf Fechan Reservoir to Dol-y-Gaer, plus visits to the restoration workshops. There is a picnic site at Pontsticill Reservoir and a tearoom.
🖳 www.bmr.wales **25 E6**

Pontypool and Blaenavon Railway *Blaenavon, Torfaen* The country's highest-altitude standard-gauge preserved line, with a steeper continuous gradient than any other line, running mainly steam train trips and hosting events such as Thomas the Tank Engine weekends.
🖳 www.bhrailway.co.uk **26 F3**

West Wales
Aberystwyth Rheilffordd Craig Glaid (Electric Cliff Railway) *Constitution Hill, Cliff Terrace, Aberystwyth, Ceredigion* Britain's longest cliff railway, built in Victorian times and carrying visitors to the top of Constitution Hill, with panoramic views of Aberystwyth and Cardigan Bay, a camera obscura and tearooms (see *Historic buildings*), and a nature trail and footpath to Clarach Bay.
🖳 www.aberystwythcliffrailway.co.uk **38 B4**

Gwili Railway *Bronwydd Arms Station, Carmarthen / Caerfyrddin, Carmarthenshire* A reopened Great Western Railway branch line in the stunning Carmarthenshire hills, on the route of the Carmarthen–Aberystwyth line. **21 C8**

Pendine Museum of Speed *Pendine / Pentwyn, Carmarthenshire* Museum focusing on the use of Pendine Sands for land speed record attempts and racing, overlooking the beach and displaying a number of fast vehicles. **20 F4**

Teifi Valley Railway *Station Yard, Henllan, Ceredigion* A 3km restored section of a branch line of the Great Western Railway from Carmarthen to Aberystwyth, with a steam railway, a miniature railway, a woodland theatre and walks, a GWR library, play areas and a teashop. **31 D7**

Vale of Rheidol (Cwm Rheidol) Railway *Park Avenue, Aberystwyth, Ceredigion* Narrow-gauge steam train trips through the beautiful Rheidol Valley to Devil's Bridge, on a railway that opened in 1902 to serve the lead mines and timber and passenger traffic of the valley.
🖳 www.rheidolrailway.co.uk **38 B4**

Wye Valley and Vale of Usk
Fourteen Locks Canal Centre *High Cross, Newport / Casnewydd, City and County of Newport* An Interpretation Centre tracing the growth and decline of the Brecon and Monmouthshire Canal (see above) thorough computer displays, a virtual journey, lock-working demonstrations and more, with picnic areas and walking trails. **13 E5**

Newport's Mediaeval Ship *Newport / Casnewydd, City and County of Newport* A well-preserved 15th-century ship discovered on the banks of the Usk in 2002 and thought to have traded with Portugal and the Iberian peninsula. Conservation work is expected to take a decade; the Mary Rose Trust runs open days so that the public can see work in progress. **13 E6**

Newport Transporter Bridge *Usk Way, Newport / Casnewydd, City & County of Newport* Restored bridge designed by Ferdinand Arnodin in 1906 to carry vehicles and pedestrians across the River Usk in a suspended gondola to avoid obstructing shipping. Visitor Centre. **13 E6**

Military history

Anglesey and Snowdonia
Home Front Experience *New Street, Llandudno, Conwy* A museum re-creating civilian life during WWII. **69 C5**

Regimental Museum of the Royal Welch Fusiliers *Caernarfon Castle, Caernarfon, Gwynedd* An exhibition about Wales's oldest regiment.
🖳 www.rwfmuseum.org.uk **59 B5**

Cardiff and Vale of Glamorgan
Porthcawl Museum *Old Police Station, John St, Porthcawl, Bridgend* A museum with an exhibition about the Welsh Guards, with uniforms, regalia, arms, regimental records, war mementoes, plus items tracing the social and maritime history of the area. On the first floor are works by local artists. **2 A3**

Regimental Museum of Dragoon Guards, Regimental Museum Royal Regiment of Wales and Welch Regiment Museum *Cardiff / Caerdydd, Cardiff* Three small military museums. **4 A3**

Mid Wales and Brecon Beacons
South Wales Borderers Museum *The Barracks, Brecon / Aberhonddu, Powys* A collection of pictures, uniforms, medals and relics covering the 24th Regiment of South Wales Borderers and their three centuries of service. **25 B5**

West Wales
Gun Tower *Front St, Pembroke Dock / Doc Penfro, Pembrokeshire* A Martello tower built in 1851 to protect Pembroke's naval dockyard. It contains cannons as well as other historical artefacts.
🖳 www.pembroke-dock.co.uk **17 D5**

Wye Valley and Vale of Usk
Roman Legionary Museum *High St, Caerleon / Caerllion, City and County of Newport* A museum examining all aspects of a Roman soldier's life, from fighting to leisure activities and religious beliefs, with life-size models and an interactive children's area. **13 D6**

Royal Monmouthshire Royal Engineers Regimental Museum *Monmouth Castle, Monmouth / Trefynwy, Monmouthshire* The regiment's museum located in Great Castle House, constructed by the Marquis of Worcester in 1673 from the stones of a castle built on this site soon after the Norman invasion of 1066 to guard river crossings to the Forest of Dean, Celtic Gwent and Archenfield.
🖳 www.monmouthcastlemuseum.org.uk **27 E8**

Local history
See also Canolfan Y Barcud Kite Centre (*Animal attractions*); Haverfordwest Castle; Raglan Castle (both *Castles*); Cyfarthfa Castle and Park (*Houses and gardens*); Merlin's Hill (*Monuments and ancient sites*); Porthcawl Museum (*Military history*).

Anglesey and Snowdonia
Amgueddfa Syr Henry Jones Museum *Llangernyw, Conwy* A museum about rural life in Wales, including Henry Jones and his strugg for education, set in a restored cottag garden. **69 F7**

Conwy Mussel Museum *Conwy, Conwy* The history of pearl fishing in the area from Roman times, plus demonstrations of mussel harvesting today. **69 D5**

Holyhead Maritime Museum *New Beach, Holyhead / Caergybi, Isle of Anglesey* A museum about the histor of seafaring in the area, in reputedly the oldest lifeboat house in Wales (c.1858). **66 C1**

Llandudno Museum *Chardon Hous 17-19 Gloddaeth Street, Llandudno, Conwy* A museum charting how the town developed as a resort. Other displays include a Roman tile with a footprint, a recreated Welsh kitchen and paintings and sculptures from around the world. **69 C5**

Llanrwst Almshouses *Llanrwst, Conwy* A new museum about everyd life in a Welsh market town, created from almshouses established in 1610. **60 B4**

Lloyd George Museum and Highgate Cottage *Llanystumdwy, Gwynedd* The childhood home of British Prime Minister David Lloyd George, now housing a museum dedicated to his life and times, a Victorian garden and a shoemaker's workshop. **52 A1**

National Slate Museum / Amgueddfa Cymru *Padarn Country Park, Llanberis, Gwynedd* The history of slate quarrying in North Wales, wit machinery and railway equipment, a waterwheel, slate-splitting and iron forging demonstrations, a cinema and photographs.
🖳 https://museum.wales/slate **59 B7**

Oriel Môn *Rhosmeirch, Isle of Anglesey* A purpose-built museum with a Heritage Gallery relating the cultural history of Anglesey and an ar gallery exhibiting work in all media. **67 D6**

Cardiff and Vale of Glamorgan
Cosmeston Medieval Village *Cosmeston Lakes Country Park, Lavernock Rd, Penarth, Vale of Glamorgan* A 14th-century village reconstructed on its original site, with medieval buildings and gardens, a

hall museum, rare livestock breeds, ...stumed farmworkers and guides, ...d special events such as jousting and ...chery. **4 C3**

...owbridge Museum *Town Hall, ...owbridge / Y Bont Faen, Vale of ...amorgan* A local history museum ...two blocks of cells dating from ...e building's time as a house of ...rrection, with exhibits ranging from ...on Age to Victorian times. **3 B6**

...Fagans National Museum of ...istory *St Fagans / Sain Fagan, Cardiff* ...n open-air museum tracing centuries ...Welsh culture, industry and ...ostume. ⌨https://museum.wales/ ...fagans **4 A2**

...lid Wales and Brecon Beacons

...recknock Museum and Art Gallery *...aptain's Walk, Brecon / Aberhonddu, ...owys* A museum in the early-Victorian ...ire Hall, with displays on prehistoric ...mes and the Dark Ages, rural life, and ...atural history (including studies by ...dwardian naturalists). The art gallery ...xhibits recent work from Wales. **5 B5**

...owell Harris Museum *Coleg ...efeca, College Lane, Trefeca, ...owys* A museum on the history of ...e Methodists in Wales, the life and ...ork of Howel Harris and the Trefeca ...ommunity. **25 A7**

...anidloes Museum of Local ...istory and Industry *Town Hall, ...reat Oak St, Llanidloes, Powys* A ...useum about the development of ...anidloes over the last 300 years, ...cluding its mining and woollen ...dustries and the Chartist movement, ...us a Natural History gallery on the ...rests of Britain. **40 B4**

...ewtown Textile Museum *...–7 Commercial St, Newtown / ...Drenewydd, Powys* A museum in ...n early 19th-century weaving shop ...nd weavers' cottages, recording ...e history of the woollen industry in ...ewtown. **47 E6**

...owysland Museum and ...ontgomery Canal Centre *...anal Wharf, Severn St, Welshpool / ...Trallwng, Powys* A museum on the ...story of mid Wales from the earliest ...rehistoric settlers, including displays ...n archaeology, agriculture, the dev-...opment of canal and railway systems, ...nd social history. Canal and town ...ails are available on request. **47 B8**

...adnorshire Museum *Temple St, ...andrindod Wells / Llandrindod, Powys* ... museum about the development of ...e spa town, with additional displays ...f archaeological discoveries, artefacts ...elating to rural life, and images. **41 F6**

...obert Owen Museum *The Cross, ...road St, Newtown / Y Drenewydd, ...owys* A museum about Socialist ...obert Owen, born here in 1771 ...nd the inspiration behind the ...o-operative movement, including ...any of his letters. **47 E6**

Lake Vyrnwy Sculpture Trail
Portfolioryanfoster Dreamstime

North East Wales

Ceiriog Memorial Institute *Glyn Ceiriog, Wrexham* A memorial to local poet John 'Ceiriog' Hughes and other notable Welsh people, with a collection of memorabilia. **55 A9**

Old Gaol *Ruthin / Rhuthun, Denbighshire* A new attraction based around Ruthin's Victorian prison, much of which has been preserved, including the baths, well, cell lighting and clock. **62 C3**

Rhyl Museum and Arts Centre *Church Street, Rhyl / Y Rhyl, Denbighshire* The history of the town as a seaside resort, plus displays on other topics, including the submarine 'Resurgam' and photography. **70 C2**

Wrexham County Borough Museum *Regent Street, Wrexham / Wrecsam, Wrexham* A former militia barracks hosting exhibitions about the region since the Bronze Age. **63 D7**

Swansea, Gower and Vale of Neath

Cefn Coed Colliery Museum *Aberdulais, Neath Port Talbot* A museum in the former Cefn Coed Colliery, featuring a steam winding engine (now electrically driven) and old mining tools and equipment. **10 C2**

Dylan Thomas Centre *Old Guildhall, Somerset Place, Swansea / Abertawe, Swansea* A permanent exhibition on Swansea's famous son, in a centre also hosting the Ty Llen programme of year-round literary events. **9 D8**

Egypt Centre *University of Wales Swansea, Swansea / Abertawe, Swansea* A museum housing 3,500 items from the collection of Egyptian antiquities amassed by pharmacist Sir Henry Wellcome, including a 21st Dynasty coffin and some cosmetic palettes. ⌨www.egypt.swan.ac.uk **9 D8**

Gower Heritage Centre *Parkmill, Swansea* A museum of rural life and crafts based around a working 12th-century watermill. ⌨www. gowerheritagecentre.co.uk **9 E5**

National Waterfront Museum *Maritime Quarter, Swansea / Abertawe, Swansea* A new museum about Wales's industrial and maritime heritage, with state-of-the-art interactive displays in a listed former warehouse overlooking a collection of historic ships. ⌨https://museumwales.ac.uk **9 D8**

South Wales Miners Museum *Afan Argoed Visitor Centre, Afan Forest Park, Cynonville, Neath Port Talbot* A small museum depicting the lives of miners and their families in the valleys of south Wales. ⌨www.swminers.co.uk **10 C3**

▼ Pontcysyllte Aqueduct
Nigel Hoy / Dreamstime

Swansea Museum *Victoria Rd, Maritime Quarter, Swansea / Abertawe, Swansea* Wales's oldest museum, with local artefacts, such as a rare porcelain teapot, old photographs and paintings, and a reconstructed Welsh kitchen, plus more exotic displays, including an Egyptian mummy and an Ichthyosaur skeleton. ⌨www.swanseamuseum.co.uk/ **9 D8**

Valleys of South Wales

Cynon Valley Museum *Depot Rd, Gadlys, Aberdare / Aberdâr, Rhondda Cynon Taff* A museum on the history of the Cynon Valley, with an emphasis on coal mining and the 1984–5 miners' strike, with multimedia displays in Welsh and English. **11 B7**

Nantgarw China Works Museum *Nantgarw, Treforest, Rhondda Cynon Taff* A museum about the history of the china works, with displays of Billingsley porcelain and demonstrations by craftspeople. ⌨https:// nantgarwchinaworksmuseum.co.uk **12 E2**

Pontypridd Historical and Cultural Centre *Pontypridd, Rhondda Cynon Taff* A museum tracing the history of the town, with displays of agricultural and industrial implements, a working model of the railway station and the reconstructed dressing room of local opera singer Sir Geraint Evans. **11 E8**

Rhondda Heritage Park *Lewis Merthyr Colliery, Coed Cae Rd, Trehafod, Pontypridd, Rhondda Cynon Taff* A museum about the importance of coal mining to the south Wales valleys and to Welsh heritage and culture, with a cage ride to the pit bottom and a Visitor Centre with exhibitions and video displays. **11 D7**

Torfaen Museum *Park Buildings, Pontypool / Pont-y-pŵl, Torfaen* A museum with permanent and temporary exhibitions on the valley's history, housed in a Georgian stable block with an outdoor performance area hosting Shakespeare, Welsh poetry readings and more. **13 B5**

West Wales

Amgueddfa Ceredigion Aberystwyth *Coliseum, Terrace Road, Aberystwyth, Ceredigion* A museum in a restored Edwardian theatre, with displays on archaeology, local folk life, agriculture, crafts such as spinning and weaving, lead-mining, clocks, seafaring and more. There are also temporary art exhibitions. ⌨https:// ceredigionmuseum.wales **38 B4**

Amgueddfa Ceredigion Cei Newydd *Heritage Centre, Glyn Square, New Quay / Ceinewydd, Ceredigion* A small museum on local and natural history. ⌨https:// ceredigionmuseum.wales **31 A7**

Amgueddfa Ceredigion Llanbedr Pont Steffan *County Library, Lampeter / Llanbedr Pont Steffan, Ceredigion* Displays on local history in the library foyer. **32 C4**

Amgueddfa Ceredigion Tregaron *Yr Hen Ysgol, Tregaron, Ceredigion* Small local history exhibitions. ⌨https://ceredigionmuseum.wales **39 F6**

Carmarthenshire County Museum *Abergwili, Carmarthenshire* A museum tracing Carmarthenshire's history, with displays on archaeology, pottery, furniture, costume, farm life and World War II, plus a reconstructed Victorian schoolroom and portraits, landscape paintings. It is housed in a former palace of the bishops of St David's; visitors can see the bishops' private chapel and the Bishop's Pond, a Site of Special Scientific Interest housing dragonflies and herons and circled by a footpath. ⌨https://cofgar.wales **22 C1**

Llyfrgell Genedlaethol Cymru (National Library of Wales) *Penglais, Aberystwyth, Ceredigion* The biggest library in Wales and the national legal deposit library holding over 6 million books. It hosts changing exhibitions and the permanent 'A Nation's Heritage', including treasures from the library's collection of early books, manuscripts, paintings and maps from Wales and the other Celtic countries. ⌨www.llgc.org.uk **38 B4**

Milford Haven Museum *Milford Marina, Milford Haven / Aberdaugleddau, Pembrokeshire* A museum about Milford's past, including its maritime history, in a converted quayside warehouse. ⌨www.milfordhavenmuseum.co.uk **16 C4**

Narberth Museum *Narberth / Arberth, Pembrokeshire* A museum detailing market town life a century ago, with costumes,

▲ Rhondda Heritage Park
Sarah Smith / Dreamstime

photographs and other memorabilia, and special exhibits on local business, education, entertainment and military matters. The research room has an archive of local books and old photographs. ⌨www.narberthmuseum.co.uk **20 E2**

National Coracle Centre *Cenarth, Ceredigion* A unique collection of coracles (small roundish boats made from waterproofed hides) from Wales, the Middle East and elsewhere, plus coracle-making displays. The visit includes a restored 17th-century flour mill, and there are excellent views of the salmon-leap waterfalls at Cenarth (see *Towns and Villages*). ⌨www. visitpembrokeshire.com **31 D5**

Parc Howard Museum and Art Gallery *Felinfoel Rd, Llanelli, Carmarthenshire* A museum with a collection of Llanelli pottery and other material related to the history of the town, plus artworks, in a house built by the Buckley brewing family in 1885 and surrounded by a 27-acre park. https://cofgar.wales **8 B5**

Tenby Museum and Art Gallery *Castle Hill, Tenby / Dinbych-y-Pysgod, Pembrokeshire* An award-winning museum with permanent displays on the maritime and social history of Tenby and South Pembrokeshire from the Stone Age to the present, plus archaeology and geology. The Wilfred Harrison Art Gallery houses works by Augustus John, Gwen John, Nina Hamnet and other artists. ⌨www.tenbymuseum.org.uk **17 D8**

Wye Valley and Vale of Usk

Abergavenny Museum *Castle St, Abergavenny / Y Fenni, Monmouthshire* A museum in the grounds of Abergavenny Castle (see *Castles*), with exhibitions on local history, including a reconstructed Victorian farmhouse kitchen and a saddler's workshop, and children's activities. ⌨www. abergavennymuseum.co.uk **26 E4**

Chepstow Museum *Bridge St, Chepstow / Cas-Gwent, Monmouthshire* A museum about the once-important port and market centre and its industries, including shipbuilding and salmon fishing, in an 18th-century merchant's house. ⌨www.monlife.co.uk **14 D2**

Goytre Wharf Heritage, Activity and Study Centre *Llanover, Monmouthshire* An eight-acre site on the Brecon and Monmouthshire Canal (see *Transport*) with industrial relics dating back 200 years (including lime kilns), a marina with fish, a waterside Information and Study Centre about

▼ **Carew Tidal Mill** Helen Hotson / Dreamstime

the canal, a tramroad exhibition, canoe tours, a gallery with local paintings and other exhibits, a play area, a woodland walk and an aqueduct. **13 A6**

Newport Museum and Art Gallery *John Frost Square, Newport / Casnewydd, City and County of Newport* A museum with displays on local archaeology and social and industrial history, with a gallery of 19th- and 20th-century and contemporary British art, design and photography, including the John Wait teapot collection. There are children's events and workshops. **13 E6**

Old Station *Tintern Parva, Monmouthshire* A Visitor Centre in a Victorian station that was part of the Wye Valley Railway, with a model steam railway on summer weekends, changing exhibitions and picnic spots. **14 B2**

Usk Rural Life Museum *Malt Barn, New Market St, Usk / Brynbuga, Monmouthshire* A museum about life in the Welsh borders from Victorian times to 1950. **13 B7**

Factories, mills and mines

Anglesey and Snowdonia

Great Orme Bronze Age Copper Mines *Great Orme Country Park, Llandudno, Conwy* An old metal mine with 3500-year-old passages leading to a prehistoric cavern and a Visitor Centre with displays about Bronze Age life and archaeological artifacts. **68 C5**

Inigo Jones Slateworks *Groeslon, Gwynedd* The last fully operational slateworks in North Wales. 🖳www.inigojones.co.uk **58 C5**

Llechwedd Slate Caverns *Blaenau Ffestiniog, Gwynedd* Guided tours of an old slate quarry by former miners, including the Deep Mine, accessed via the steepest funicular railway in Britain, plus a re-created Victorian village. **60 E2**

Sygun Copper Mine *Beddgelert, Gwynedd* A re-creation of the life of Victorian miners in Snowdonia National Park, with tours of the old workings, tunnels and chambers. 🖳www.syguncoppermine.co.uk **59 E8**

Cardiff and Vale of Glamorgan

Cefn Cribwr Ironworks *Bedford Park, Cefn Cribwr, Bridgend* One of the most complete buildings of its kind in the country, a Scheduled Ancient Monument, with interpretative panels taking visitors through the iron-making process. The well-preserved remains of the calcining kilns, blast-furnace and other structures are still visible. **10 F4**

North East Wales

Minera Lead Mines and Country Park *Wern Road, Minera, Wrexham* The remnants of a 19th-century lead mine, a reconstructed engine house and a visitor centre with displays on the geology and social and industrial history of lead mining in the area, including during Roman times. **63 D6**

Valleys of South Wales

Big Pit *Brynmawr Rd, Blaenavon, Torfaen* An 1880 colliery with tours led by ex miners to the pit floor with its historic mine workings, and original buildings housing exhibitions. 🖳https://museumwales.ac.uk **26 F2**

Blaenavon Industrial Landscape *North St, Blaenavon, Torfaen* A World Heritage Site with western Europe's best-preserved 18th-century ironworks, including working models and restored ironworkers' cottages. 🖳https://cadw.gov.wales **26 F3**

Llanyrafon Mill *Llanyrafon Way, Cwmbran / Cwmbrân, Torfaen* A rare surviving triple stone watermill, dating from the 17th century and housing historic local artefacts. **13 C5**

Sirhowy Ironworks *Sirhowy, Blaenau Gwent* The ruins of the area's first coke-fired furnace, built in 1778. **25 F7**

The Winding House *White Rose Way, New Tredegar / Tredegar Newydd, Caerphilly* The restored east winding house and huge steam winding engine of a large 19th-century colliery, with displays on the history of local coal mining. **12 B2**

Ynysfach Engine House *Merthyr Tydfil / Merthyr Tudful, Merthyr Tydfil* The restored blast-engine house and four furnaces of an early-19th-century ironworks, with a Heritage Centre with exhibitions, life-size models and an audio-visual show, 'The Story of Iron in Merthyr Tydfil', in Welsh and English. **11 A7**

West Wales

Amgueddfa'r Diwydiant Gwlan (National Wool Museum) *Drefach, Ceredigion* A museum tracing the development of the Welsh wool industry, with displays of carding, spinning and weaving by hand and on machines dating from 1855. As well as a working mill, there is a textile gallery and picnic site. 🖳https://museum.wales **31 E7**

Carew Tidal Mill *Carew, Pembrokeshire* A restored 19th-century corn mill (Wales's only intact tidal mill), containing an exhibition on the history of milling. 🖳www.carewcastle.com **17 D6**

Dolaucothi Goldmines *Old Coach House, Pumpsaint, Llanwrda, Carmarthenshire* A Roman gold mine overlooking the lovely Cothi Valley, managed by the National Trust and with an exhibition of 1930s mining equipment, audio-visual presentations, an activity room where children can pan for gold, waymarked walks, cycle hire and guided tours. Nearby are the remains of wooden Flavian fort built c.AD120 to guard the mine. 🖳www.nationaltrust.org.uk **33 D6**

Dyfi Furnace *Eglwysfach, Ceredigion* A largely intact mid-18th-century charcoal-fired furnace and charcoal store where iron ore was smelted, with a restored waterwheel and scenic waterfall. 🖳https://cadw.gov.wales **44 D4**

Rock Mills Woollen and Water Mill *Capel Dewi, Ceredigion* A weaving mill established in 1890 by John Morgan, whose descendants still produce fabrics here on machinery powered by a waterwheel. **32 D2**

Silver Mountain Experience *Llywernog, Ponterwyd, Ceredigion* The chambers where Welsh and Cornish miners blasted out lead and silver ore by candlelight in the late 18th century, with an award-winning exhibition including video presentations, waterwheels, machinery, a panning area, a heritage trail and a narrow-gauge tramway ride. 🖳www.silverminetours.co.uk **39 B7**

Y Felin Mill *St Dogmaels / Llandudoch, Pembrokeshire* One of two working watermills in Wales, dating from the 12th century and still producing traditional stoneground flour. Guided tours are available, and there is a tearoom. **30 C3**

Food and drink

Cardiff and Vale of Glamorgan

Llanerch Vineyard *Hensol, Pendoylan, Vale of Glamorgan* Wales's largest vineyard, producing award-winning wines, with a tasting area, seven acres of vines and a small country park of gardens, woodland and lakes. **3 A8**

West Wales

Cwm Deri Vineyard *Martletwy, Pembrokeshire* A vineyard in 'the valley of oaks', producing wines, liqueurs and mead. 🖳www.cwm-deri.co.uk **17 B6**

Pant Mawr Farm *Rosebush, Maenclochog, Pembrokeshire* A working farm producing award-winning handmade cheese, including Caws Cerwyn, named after the highest mountain in the Preseli range. **20 B1**

Wye Valley and Vale of Usk

Sugar Loaf Vineyard *Dummar Farm, Pentre Lane, Abergavenny / Y Fenni, Monmouthshire* A 5-acre vineyard on the gentle, south-facing Sugar Loaf, producing award-winning Welsh wine from 7 grape varieties. Wine tastings and vineyard tours are available. **26 D3**

General museums

Anglesey and Snowdonia

Teapot World *Castle Street, Conwy, Conwy* Novelty and humorous teapots ranging in date from the mid-18th century to the present. **69 D5**

Sport

Activity centres

See also individual activities below

Mid Wales and Brecon Beacons

Llangorse Multi Activity Centre *Gilfach Farm, Llangorse, Powys* A large activity centre with indoor natural rock faces, facilities for bouldering, pot-holing, hill walking, abseiling, canoeing, biking, riding in the Brecon Beacons, and more. 🖳www.activityuk.com **25 B7**

Parkwood Outdoors *Dolygaer Near Merthyr Tydfil / Merthyr Tudful* An outdoor activity centre overlooking the Pontsticill Reservoir, hosting a range of activities, including gorge-walking, abseiling, hiking, canoeing and stand-up paddle boarding. 🖳https://dolygaeroutdoor.co.uk **25 E6**

West Wales

Celtic Quest Coasteering *Abereiddy beach, Pembrokeshire / Sir Benfro* A specialist in coasteering, hosting cliff jumping, caving, and adventure swimming activities. Sessions run twice daily from May–October. www.celticquestcoasteering.com **18 C3**

Climbing and caving

Anglesey and Snowdonia

Plas-y-Brenin National Mountain Centre *Capel Curig, Conwy* Mountaineering, rock climbing, canoeing and orienteering courses at the National Centre for mountain activities. 🖳www.pyb.co.uk **60 C2**

Valleys of South Wales

Rock UK – Summit Centre *Taff Bargoed, Trelewis, Treharris, Merthyr Tydfil* An indoor climbing and tuition centre close to the Brecon Beacons, with facilities for climbers, from beginners to the experienced, including one of Europe's biggest indoor climbing walls and an indoor cave. Outdoor activities are also offered. 🖳rockuk.org/centres/summit-centre **12 C2**

Cycling

See also *Walking, riding and cycling trails*.

Anglesey and Snowdonia

Antur Stiniog *Llechwedd Slate Caverns, Blaenau Ffestiniog* An uplift assisted MTB centre with 14 trails that range from novice to professional, graded from green to black. Bike hire available plus cafe and bike shop. 🖳www.anturstiniog.com **60 E2**

Valleys of South Wales

BikePark Wales *Abercanaid, Merthyr Tydfil / Merthyr Tudful* UK's premier mountain biking destination, with dozens of trails for raiders of every level. There are also coaching services, a vehicular uplift, café, and well-stocked bike shop. 🖳www.bikeparkwales.com **11 B8**

Wye Valley and Vale of Usk

Geraint Thomas National Velodrome of Wales *Spytty Park, Newport / Casnewydd, City and County of Newport* A new multimillion-pound high-speed cycling track attracting world-class riders. **13 E6**

Horseracing

Wye Valley and Vale of Usk

Chepstow Racecourse *Chepstow / Cas-Gwent, Monmouthshire* A prestigious racecourse with year-round National Hunt and Flat racing, including the Welsh Grand National. 🖳www.chepstow-racecourse.co.uk **14 C2**

Motorsports

Valleys of South Wales

Taff Valley Activity Centre *Cwrt y Celyn Farm, Eglwysilan, Pontypridd, Rhondda Cynon Taff* Quad biking (adult trails, including a cross-countr nature trail, and a children's circuit), plus clay shooting, 4-wheel driving ar target shooting. 🖳www.adventurewales.co.uk **12 E**

Riding

Anglesey and Snowdonia

Snowdonia Riding Stables *Waunfawr, Gwynedd* Riding, hacking and trekking on bridleways between Snowdon and the sea. **59 C6**

Cardiff and Vale of Glamorgan

South Wales Equestrian Centre *Heol-y-Cyw, Bridgend* A British Horse Society approved centre offering ride over open mountain areas. **11 F5**

Mid Wales and Brecon Beacons

Cantref Adventure Farm *Upper Cantref Farm, Cantref, Brecon / Aberhonddu, Powys* A centre offerin pony-trekking and riding in the hills o the Brecon Beacons (see *National Par and AONBs*), with experienced guide 🖳www.cantref.com **25 B5**

West Wales

Marros Riding Centre *Marros, Pendine / Pentwyn, Carmarthenshire* One- to two-hour mountainside ride, plus beach rides on Pendine Sands. 🖳www.marros-farm.co.uk **20 F4**

Rheidol Riding Centre *Capel Bangc Ceredigion* Accompanied horse and pony rides for adults and children of a levels in the scenic Rheidol Valley. 🖳www.rheidol-riding-centre.co.uk **39 B6**

Rugby

Cardiff and Vale of Glamorgan

Principality Stadium *Westgate St, Cardiff / Caerdydd, Cardiff* Tours of the state-of-the-art stadium, home of Welsh Rugby Union. 🖳www principalitystadium.wales **4 A3**

Watersports

Anglesey and Snowdonia

Canolfan Tryweryn National Whitewater Centre *Frongoch, Gwynedd* Whitewater rafting amidst spectacular Snowdonia scenery. 🖳www.ukrafting.co.uk **61 F5**

Hafan Pwllheli Marina *Pwllheli, Gwynedd* A European Centre of Excellence in sailing, and the venue for various national and international sailing and watersports events. 🖳www.hafanpwllheli.co.uk **51 A7**

Llyn Brenig *Cerrigydrudion, Conwy* A deep artificial lake in a superb setting, with a watersports centre, a sailing club and flyfishing facilities. There's also a Visitor Centre, adventu playground and lakeside cafe plus a fleet of mountain bikes for hire. 🖳www.llynbrenigsc.org.uk **61 D7**

Swansea, Gower and Vale of Neath

Gower Coast Adventures *The Mumbles / Y Mwmbwls, Swansea* Windsurfing and kayaking in Swanse Bay, including tuition. 🖳www.gowercoastadventures.co.uk **8 E5**

Wye Valley and Vale of Usk

Llandegfedd Lake Visitor and Water Sports Centre *Coed y Paen, Pontypool / Pont-y-pwl, Monmouthshire / Sir Fynwy* A hub for health and wellbeing set in the Usk Valley, complete with water sports, fishing, walking, bird watching, a restaurant and a dog friendly café. 🖳https://llandegfedd.co.uk **13 C6**

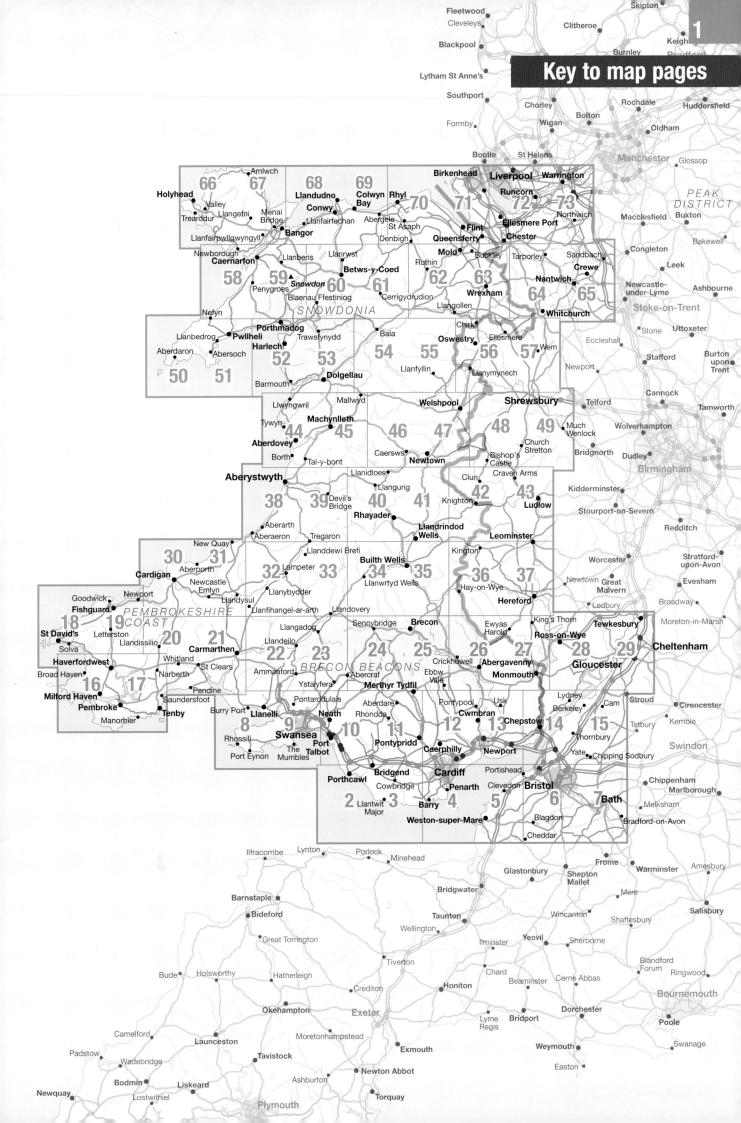

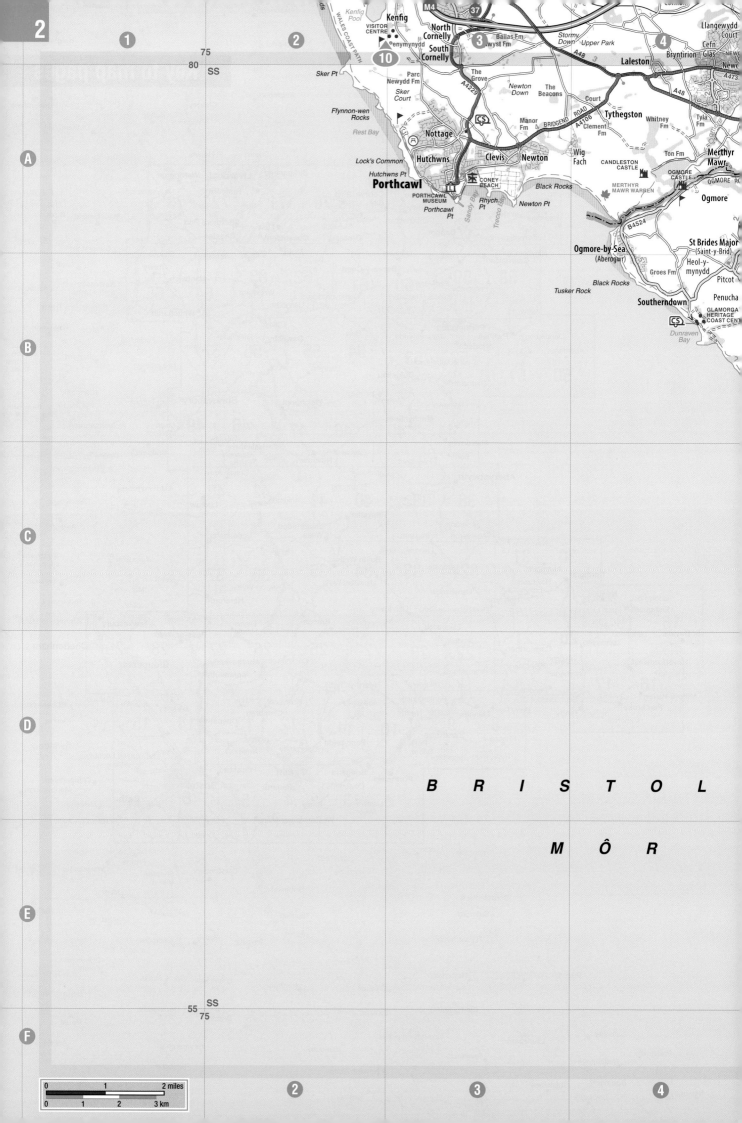

1   **2**   **3**   **4**

75

80   SS

Kenfig
Pool

Kenfig

VISITOR
CENTRE

Penymynydd

10

North
Cornelly

South
Cornelly

M4

37

Ballas Fm
wyst Fm

A48

Stormy
Down

Upper Park

Llangewydd
Court
Cefn
Glas

Bryntirion

Laleston

Newc

A473

Sker Pt

Parc
Newydd Fm

Sker
Court

A4229

The
Grove

Newton
Down

The Beacons

Manor
Fm

BRIDGEND

A4106

Clement
Fm

Court

Tythegston

Whitney
Fm

Tyla
Fm

Ffynnon-wen
Rocks

A

Rest Bay

Lock's Common

Nottage

Hutchwns

Clevis

Newton

Wig
Fach

CANDLESTON
CASTLE

MERTHYR
MAWR WARREN

Ton Fm

OGMORE
CASTLE

OGMORE RO

Merthyr
Mawr

Ogmore

Hutchwns Pt

Porthcawl

PORTHCAWL
MUSEUM

Porthcawl
Pt

CONEY
BEACH

Sandy Bay

Rhych
Pt

Trecco Bay

Black Rocks

Newton Pt

B4524

St Brides Major
(Saint-y-Brid)

Ogmore-by-Sea
(Aberogwr)

Groes Fm

Heol-y-
mynydd

Pitcot

Penucha

B

Tusker Rock

Black Rocks

Southerndown

GLAMORGA
HERITAGE
COAST CENT

Dunraven
Bay

C

D

B R I S T O L

M Ô R

E

55

SS

75

F

0   1   2 miles
0   1   2   3 km

2   **3**   **4**

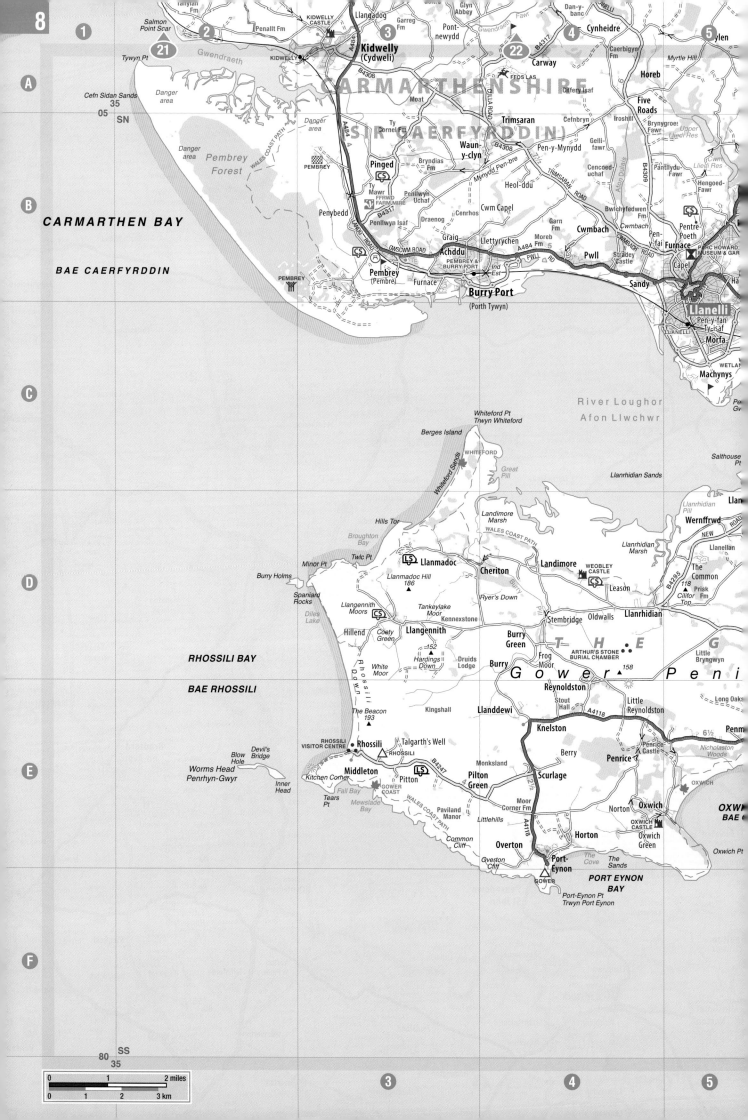

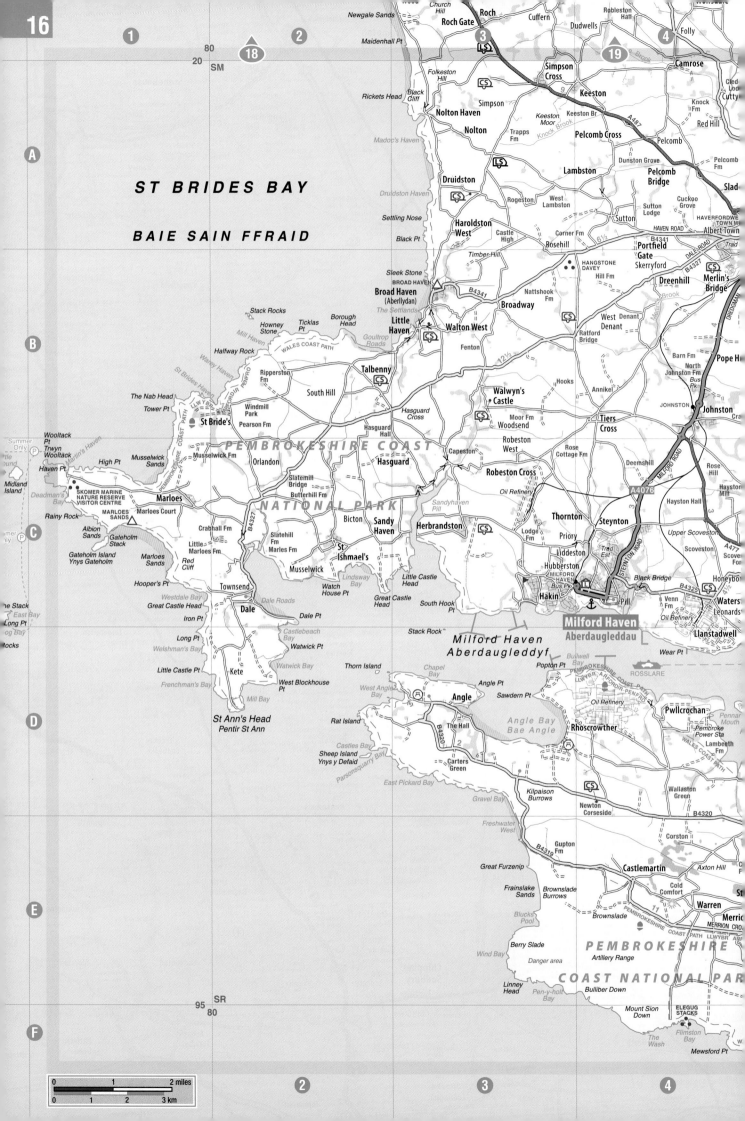

ST BRIDES BAY

BAIE SAIN FFRAID

PEMBROKESHIRE COAST

NATIONAL PARK

Milford Haven
Aberdaugleddyf

Milford Haven
Aberdaugleddau

PEMBROKESHIRE

COAST NATIONAL PARK

0   1   2 miles
0 1 2 3 km

IRISH

SEA

MÔR IWERDDON

ST BRIDES BAY

BAIE SAIN FFRAID

PEMBROKESHIRE COAST

NATIONAL PARK

Ynys Deullyn
Porth
Glastwr

Pwll Whiting
Pwll Llong
Pwll Olfa
Trwyn Llwyd

CARREG
SAMPSON
Abercastle

Trefin
(Trevine)

Trefelyn

Penclegyr
Porth-
gain
Porth Dwfn
Porth Egr

Trwyncastell
Barry
Island Fm
Abereiddi
Bay
Aber-pwll
Aberdinas
Porth Tre-wen

Porthgain

Felindre
Ho

Binchurn
Fm

Penparc

BURIAL
CHAMBER

Abereiddy
Portheiddy

Llanrhian

Llanon

3½

Cwmwdig
Water

Mesur-y-dorth

Square and
Compass

Penysgwarne
Fm

Trec
Fm

Bank Ho

A487

Western

Cleddau

Tremynydd
Fawr

Berea

Trefochlyd
Fm

Croes-goch

Trevigan

Trenewydd
Fawr

Hollybush

Rive

Penllechwen

Dduall

Waun
Beddau

Tretio

Tretio Common

Carnhedryn
Uchaf

Spite
Moor

Treglemais

Waun
Fawr

Treffynnon

Gesail-fawr

Porthgwyn

Carn Treliwyd

Llechenhinen

WALES COAST PATH

Carn Llidi
181

Carn
Hen

ST
DAVID'S

PEMBROKESHIRE COAST

Carnhedryn

Carn
Treglemaes

Abernant

Trenichol

Llanreithan

St David's Head
Penmaen Dewi

Porthmelgan

Treleddyd-
fawr

Rhodiad

Hendre

Caerfarchell

Llanhowel
Skyfog

Llanddinog

Lochmeyler

Berry Bush

North Bishop

Porthselau

Porth Lleuog
Whitesands Bay
Porth-mawr

B4583

Dowrog
Common

Mynydd du

Caerforiog

Paran

Lower
Rhosgranog

Llandeloy

Renarthur
Fm

River Alun

Caerfforiog

Tremaenhir

Treswny
Moor

NATIONAL PARK

A487

Whitchurch

Middle Mill

Rickeston
Hall

PE N

PAE M

Point St John

Rhosson

BISHOP'S
PALACE

CATHEDRAL

St David's
(Tyddewi)

Vachelich

Nine Wells

Mount
Fm

PENYCWM

Trefga
Owen

Bishops and Clerks

Trwyn-Siôn-Owen

St Justinian

Treginnis

ST NON'S
CHAPEL

St Non's
Bay

Llandruidion
Morfa Common

Prendergast

Solva
(Solfach)

Brawdy
Airfield
(disused)

Rhydygele

Knaw

Trwyn-drain-du

Carnysgubor

Porthstinian

Porthllisky

Caerfai Bay

Caer Bwdy Bay

Upper
Solva

Lower
Solva

PEMBROKESHIRE COAST

Pointz
Castle

Bus Pk

Penycwm
Newgale
Fm

Aber Mawr
RAMSEY ISLAND

Ramsey
Island
Ynys Dewi

Rhod Isaf
136

RSPB

RAMSEY
ISLAND

Aberfelin

Porthlysgi Bay

Carreg Fran

Porth Clais

A487

PATH LLWYBR ARFORDIR PENFRO

Newgale

Trwynmynachdy

Penrhyn Twll

Meini Duon

Bay Dillyn

Black Scar

Green
Scar

Dinas Fawr

Dinas Fach

Aber-west

Porthmynawyd

Pwll March

Brandy Brook

Wood

Church
Hill

Newgale Sands

Maidenhall Pt

Roch Ga

Rickets Head

Black
Cliff

Folkeston
Hill

Nolton Ha

Madoc's Haven

Druidst

16

Druidston Haven

Settling Nose

Harc
Wes

Black Pt

70
40
SM

20
70
SM

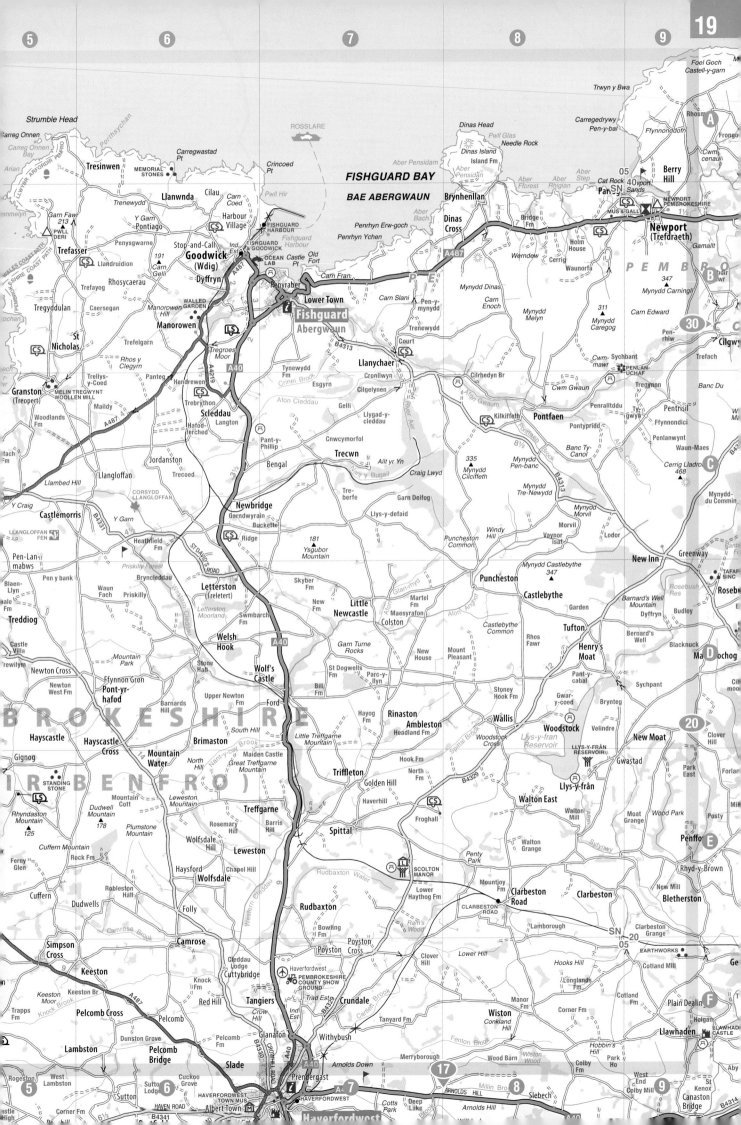

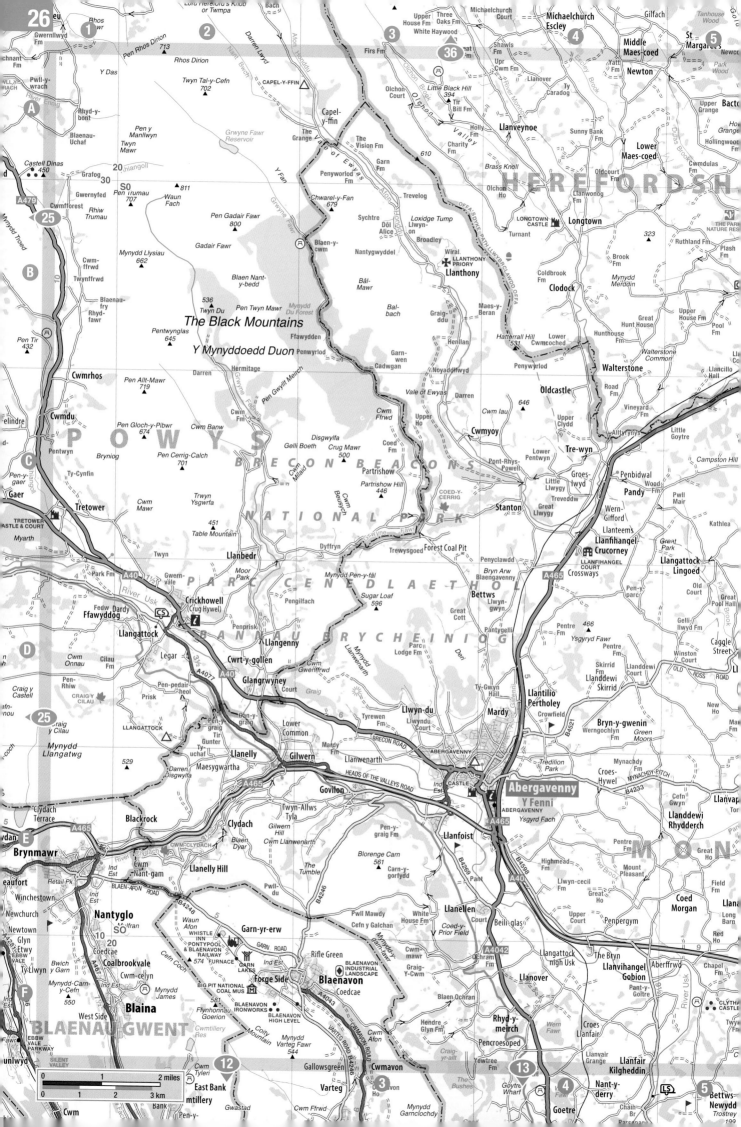

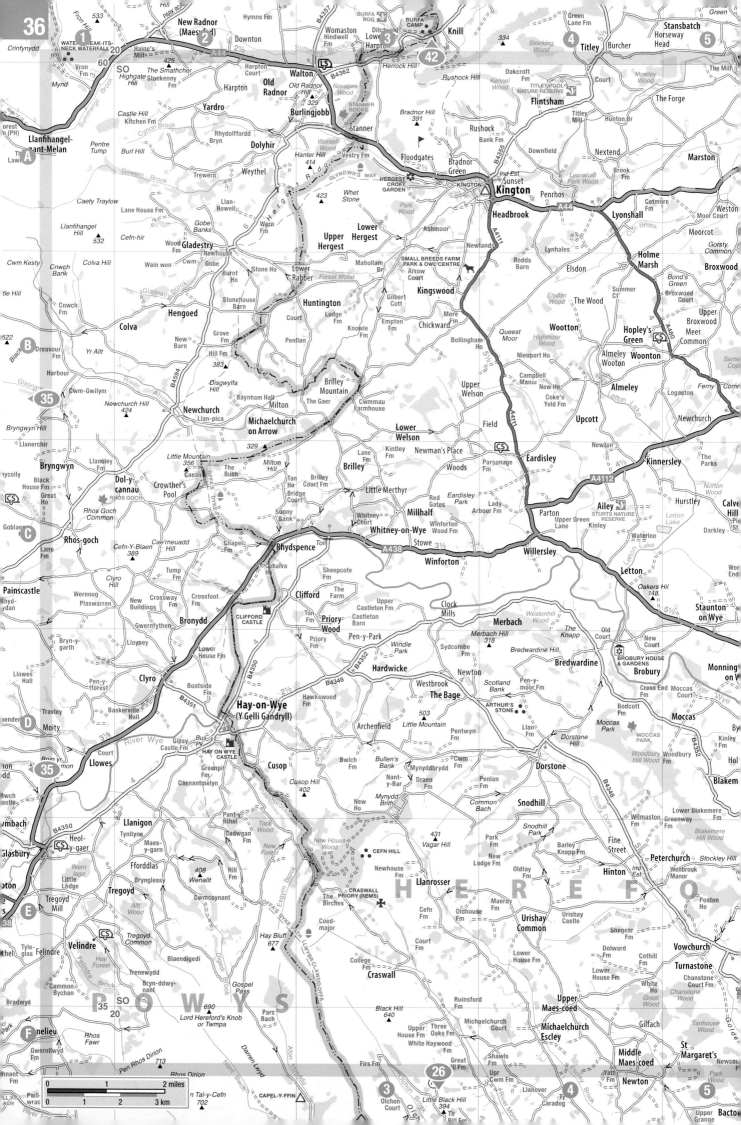

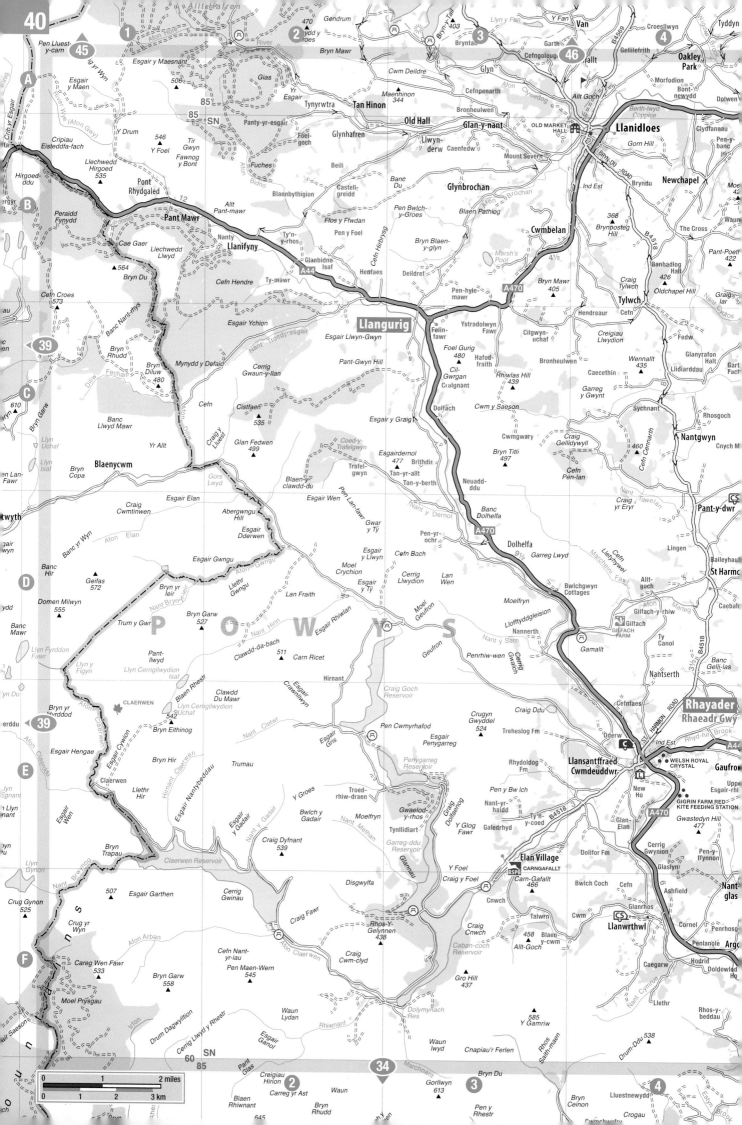

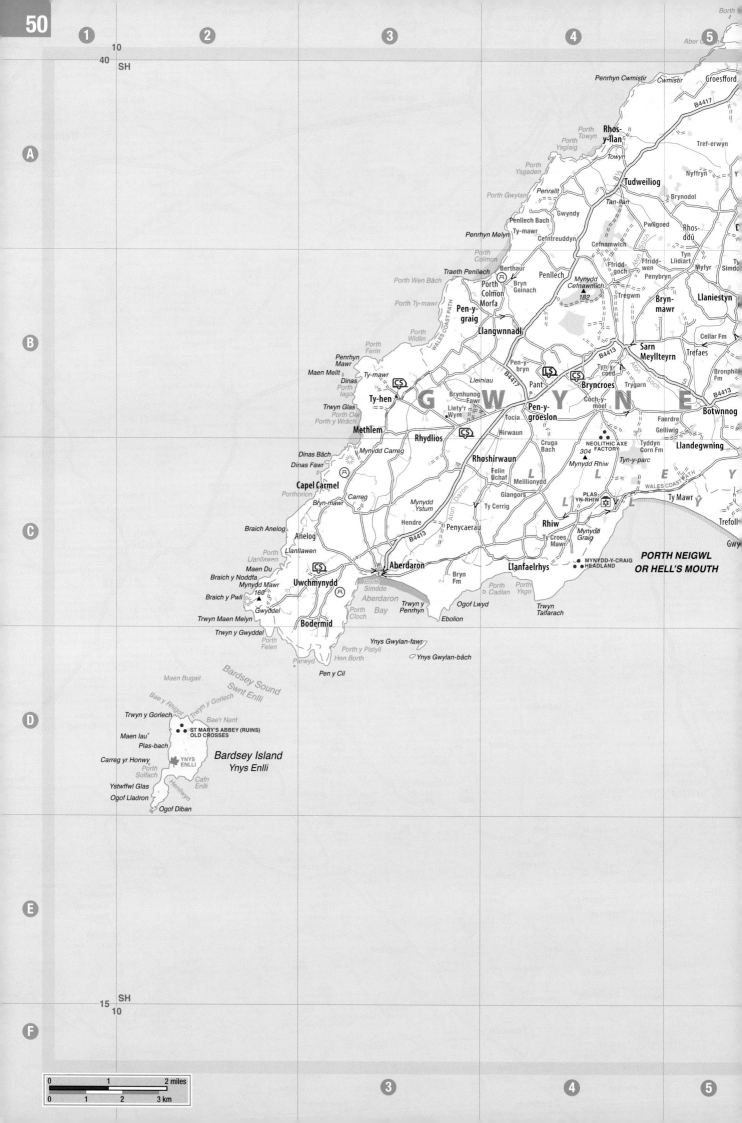

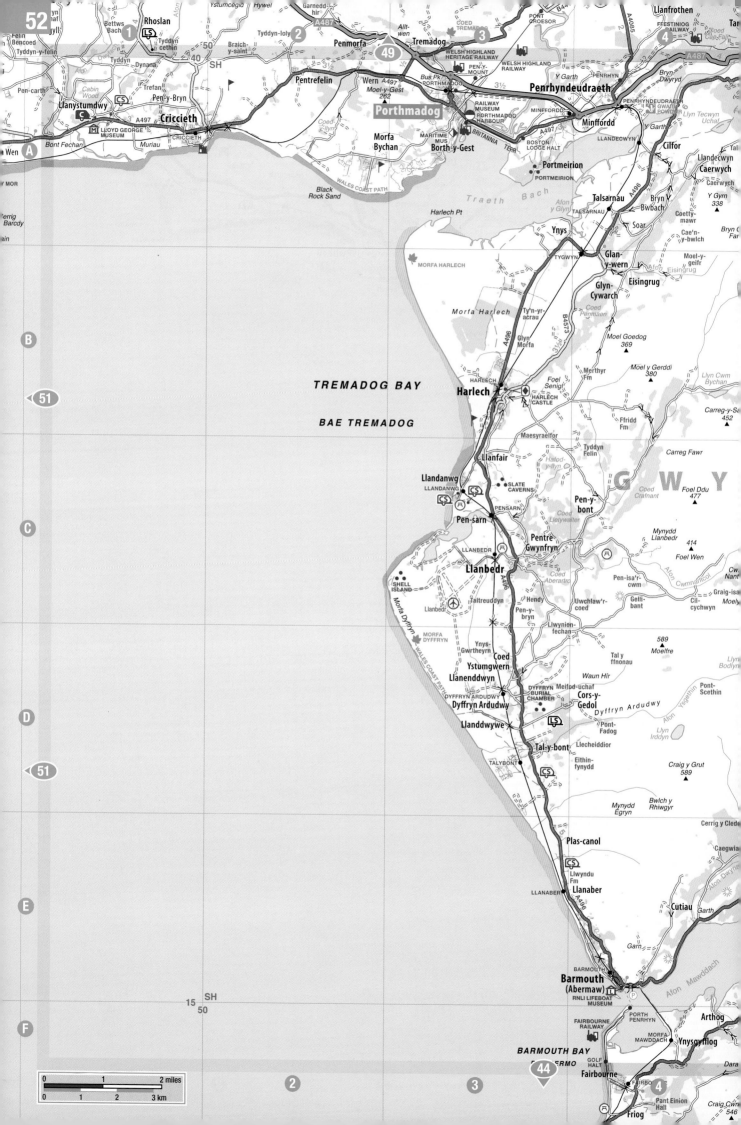

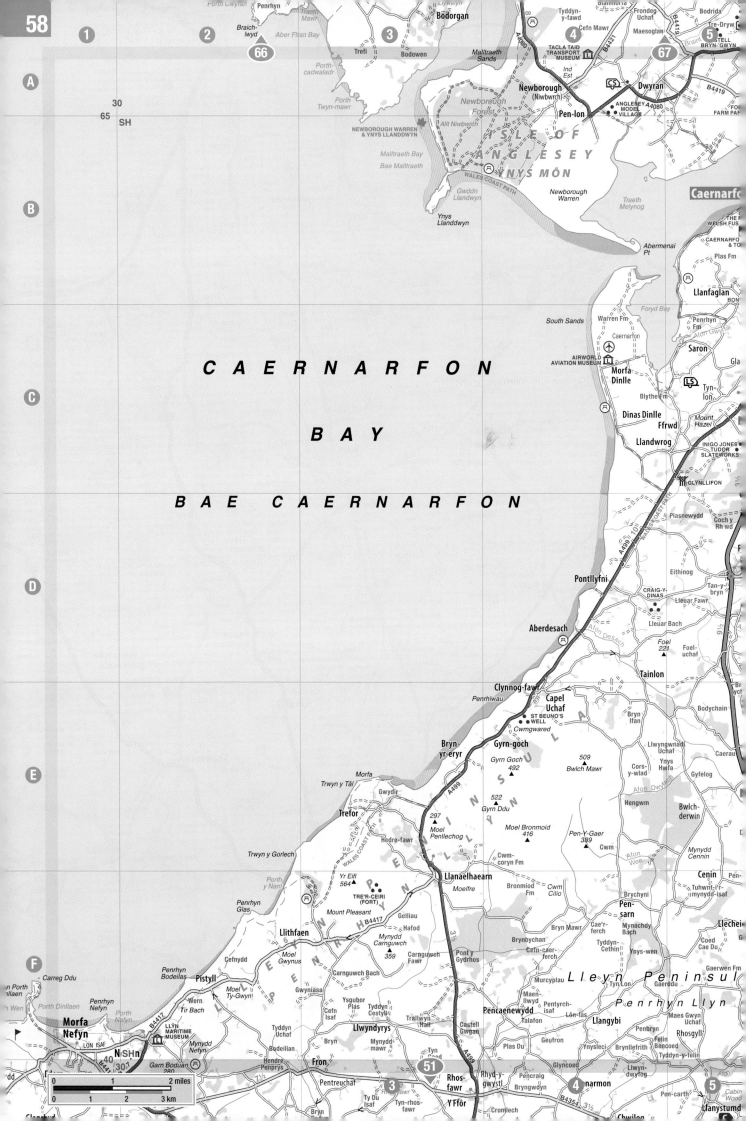

CAERNARFON

BAY

BAE CAERNARFON

ISLE OF ANGLESEY
YNYS MÔN

Caernarfon

Lleyn Peninsul
Penrhyn Llyn

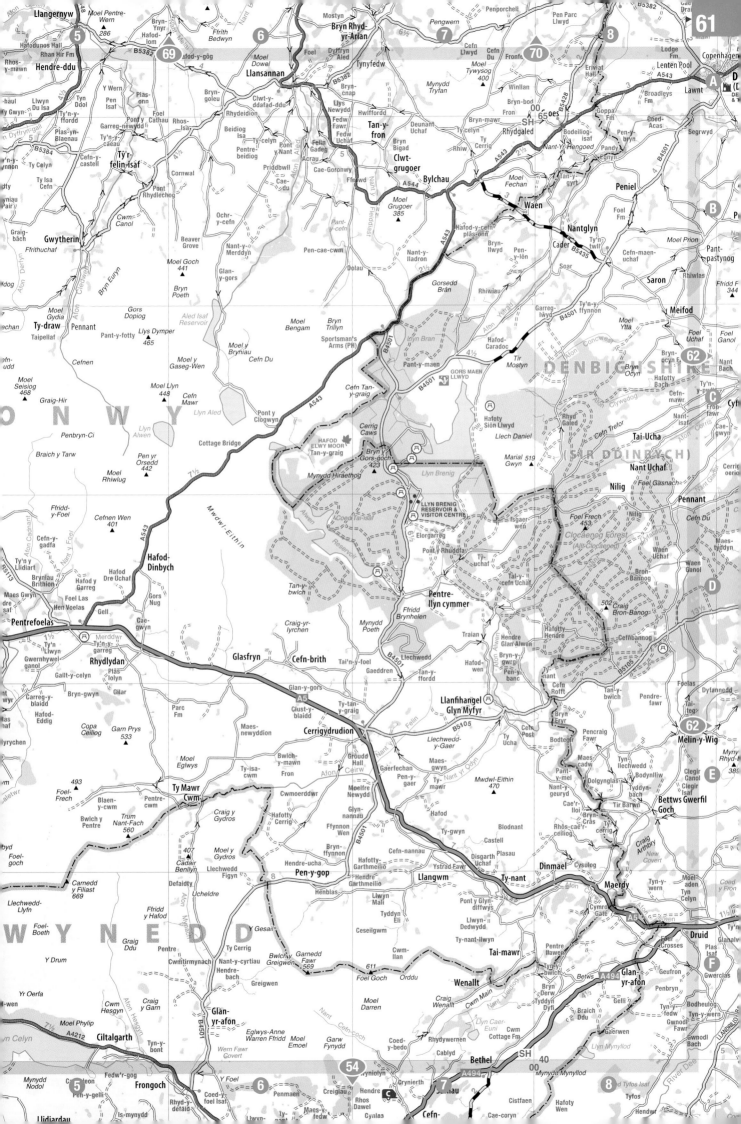

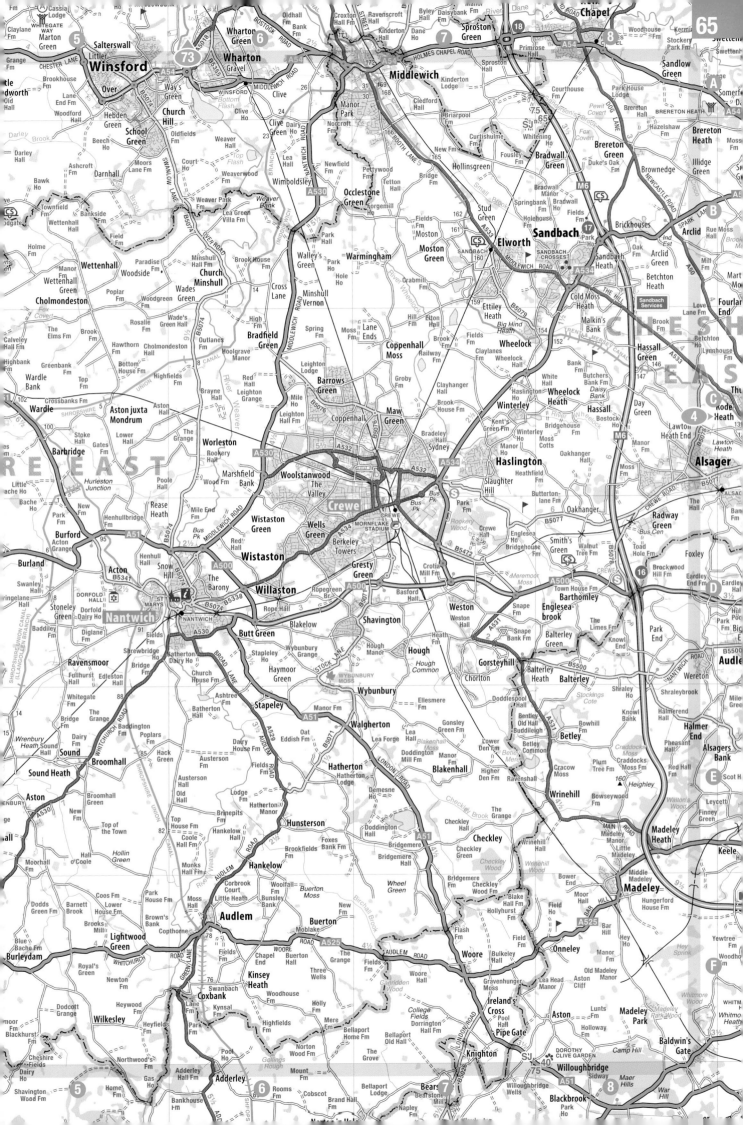

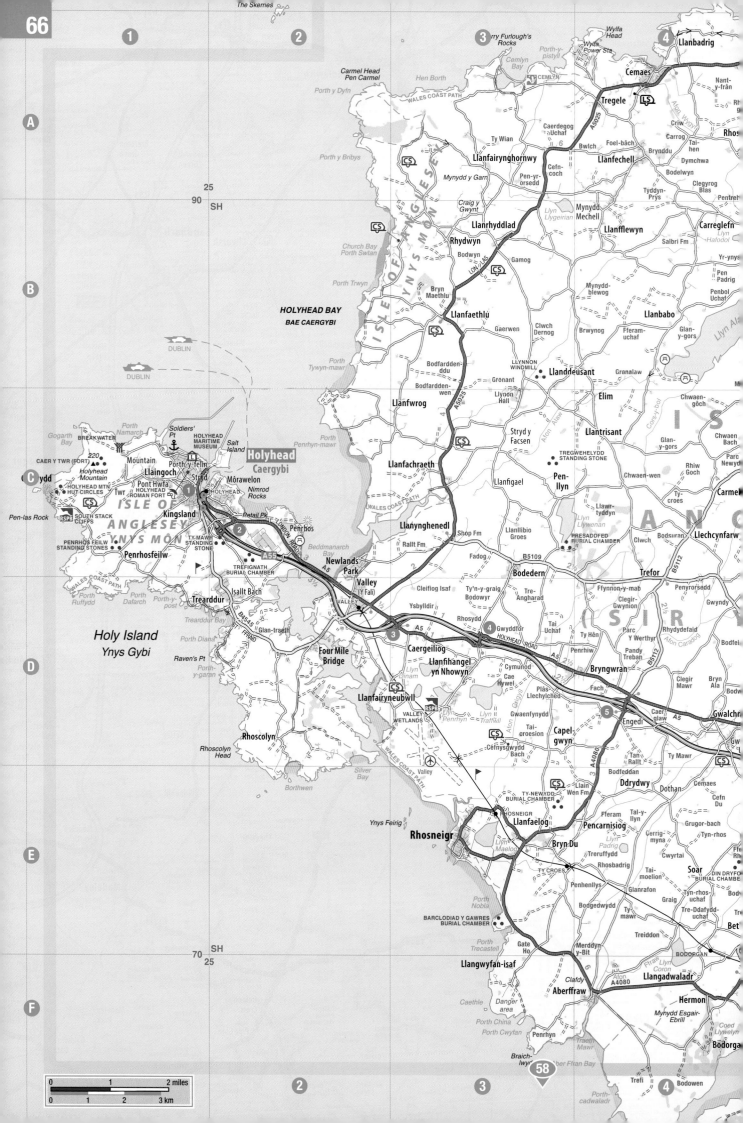

CONWY BAY
BAE CONWY

Puffin Island or
Priestholm Ynys Seiriol

Great Orm
Pen-y-Gog
Hornby Cave
GREAT
ORME
GREAT ORME
RAILWAY
GREAT ORME
COPPER MINE
Llandud

Fedw Fawr
Mariandyrys
Penhwnllys
Cefn
Bryn Ddol
Glan-
yr-afon
Caim
PENMON
PRIORY
Penmon
Outer Road

Carwad
Pen-y-
bryn
Llangoed
Bryn Celyn
Rhos
Newydd
Bryn
Cogail
Llanfaes
Lavan Sands
Conwy
Sands

17
16A
16
15A
Allt-Wen
255
Penmaen-
Bach 245
247
ABERCONWY HOU
PLAS MA
CONWY
Fryars Road
Dwygyfylchi
Pensychnant
Craigyfedwen
Llechwedd

Llyn
gyiched
Bodgylched
BEAUMARIS
CASTLE
GAOL &
COURTHOUSE
B5109
ALLT GOCH FAWR
Cefn
Gallows Point
Beaumaris
Trwyn y Penrhyn

Foel Lus
362
PENMAENMAWR
Penmaenmawr
Capelulo
Llechan
Ucha
Hen-
dy
Henry
Craig Hafodwen
Penmaenan
Garizim
Bryn
Derwydd
Hafodty
Hafod

LLANFAIRFECHAN
15
Llanfairfechan
Moelfre
435
Cefn Côch
Cerrig
Gwynion
Tanrallt Fm

Nant-y-
felin
Nant-y-pandy
Garreg Fawr
356
Craig Hafodwen

Garth
Upper Bangor
Hirael
BANGOR
Abergwyngregyn
Gorddinog
A55
14
Cammarnaint
SNOWDONIA
Foel Lwyd
Tal y Fan
Coed Mawr Hall
Ty'
g

CATHEDRAL
Maesgeirchen
PENRHYN
CASTLE
ABERGWEN,
SPINNIES
Gatehouse
Bronydd
Isaf
Crymlyn
Glyn
Ffridd
Ddu
Nant
COEDYDD
ABER
NATIONAL PARK
Foel-Ganol
533
Pen
Bryn-du
Drosgl
621
Bwlch y
Ddeufaen
Rowen
ROWEN
Cae
Côch

Glan
Adda
Minffordd
Bryn
Llandegai
Tal-y-bont
A55
Marianwinllan
Pen-y-
bryn
GWYNEDD
Moel Wnion
580
PARC CENEDLAETHOL
Llyn
Anafon
Afon Tafolog
Hafoty
Gwyn
White Hart
Gorswen
Tyddyn Bach
COED
GORSWEN
Pontwg

BANGOR SERVICES
11
70
60
Rhiw Gôch
Bryn
Hall
Gyrn
542
ERYRI
Llwytmor
ABER
FALLS
Drum
770
Pen y Castell
623
Penygadair
Bwlch-
y-gaer
Llanbedr-y-
cennin
Castell

Glasinfryn
wen
Coed
Hywel
FFELLMEN ROAD
A5
Halfway Br
Tregarth
Rachub
Llanllechid
Llefn
Foel-Fras
942
Ffrith-
y-bont
Tan-y-
bwlch
Hafodygors-wen
Carreg-
y-ffordd

B4409
Ty'n y
Caean
Sling
Tanysgafell
Ind Est
Bethesda
Gerla
Moel Faban
408
Parc
Gyrn Wigau
643
758
Drosgl
Bera
Bach
Yr Aryg
877
Garnedd
Uchaf
Hafod-y-
garreg
Coedty
Res
Dolgarrog

A4244
Wae
Rhiwlas
Braichmelyn
Foel
Ganol
Yr Elen
962
Foel
Grach
Craig
y Dulyn
Clogwynyreryr
Melynllyn
Llyn Eigiau
Moel
Eilio

794
Bera Mawr

0   1   2 miles
0   1   2   3 km

Town plans

Town plan symbols · Allwedd i Symbolau Cynllun y Dref

Motorway	*Traffordd*
Primary route – dual/single carriageway	*Prif Dramwyfeydd – Ddeuol/Sengl*
A road –dual/single carriageway	*Ffordd A – Ddeuol/Sengl*
B road – dual/single carriageway	*Ffordd B – Ddeuol/Sengl*
Minor through road, one-way street	*Ffordd Arall / Stryd un Ffordd*
Pedestrian roads	*Ffyrdd Cerddwyr*
Shopping streets	*Strydoedd Siopa*
Railway	*Rheilffordd*
Tramway with tram stop	*Tramffordd gyda Gorsaf*
Railway or bus station	*Rheilffordd / Bws Gorsaf*
Shopping precinct or retail park	*Canolfan Siopa / Pentref Siopa*
Park	*Parc*

Ⓗ Hospital *Ysbyty*
Ⓟ Parking *Parcio*
Police station *Gorsaf Heddlu*
Post office *Swyddfa'r Post*

♿ Shopmobility *Shopmobility*
Bank Ⓤ Underground or metro station *Underground/Gorsaf Metro*
▲ Youth hostel *Hostel Ieuenctid*

Tourist information · Gwybodaeth i Dwristiaid

✝ Abbey or cathedral
Abaty/Eglwys Gadeiriol

🏛 Ancient monument
Henebion

🐠 Aquarium
Acwariwm

Art gallery
Oriel Gelfyddyd

Bird garden
Gardd Adar

Building of public interest
Adeilad o Ddiddordeb Gyhoeddus

Castle
Castell

Church of interest
Eglwys o Ddiddordeb

Cinema
Sinema

Garden
Gardd

Historic ship
Llong Hanesyddol

House
Tŷ

House and garden
Tŷ a Gardd

Museum
Amgueddfa

♦ Other place of interest
Mannau o Ddiddordeb Eraill

Preserved railway
Rheilffordd wedi'u Ddiogelu

Railway station
Rheilffordd Gorsaf

Roman antiquity
Hynafiaeth Rhufeinig

Theatre
Theatr

Tourist information centre
Canolfan Wybodaeth Twrisiaeth

Zoo
Sŵ

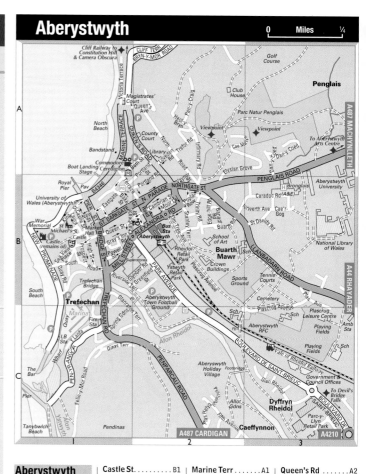

Aberystwyth

Bangor

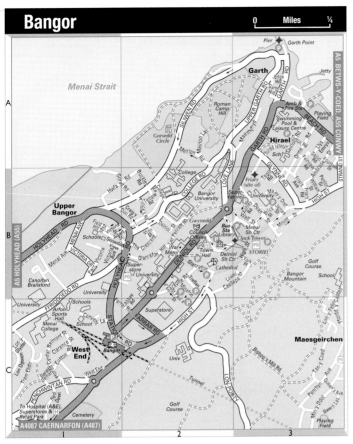

Cardiff / Caerdydd

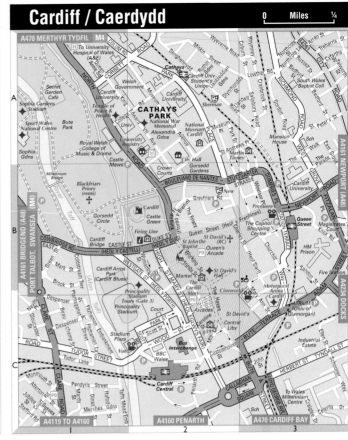

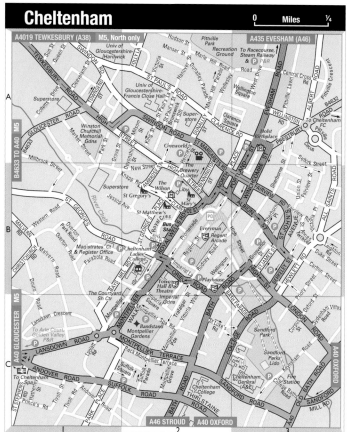

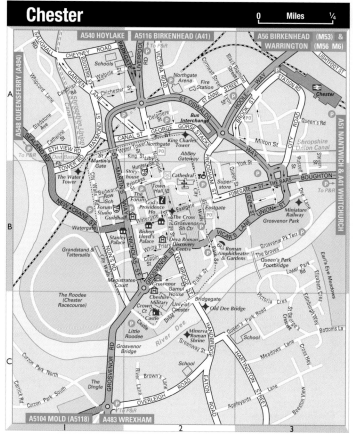

Cheltenham

Albert Rd A3
Albion St B3
All Saints Rd B3
Ambrose St A3
Andover Rd C1
Back Montpellier
Terrace C2
Bandstand ✦ C2
Bath Pde B2
Bath Rd C2
Bays Hill Rd B1
Bennington St B2
Berkeley St B2
Brewery Quarter,
The A2
Brunswick St
South A2
Bus Station B2
Carlton St B3
Central Cross Road A3
Cheltenham
College C2
Cheltenham FC A3
Cheltenham General
(A&E) Ⓗ A2
Cheltenham Ladies'
College B2
Christchurch Rd B1
Cineworld ▨ A2
Clarence Rd A2
Clarence Sq. A2
Clarence St B2
Cleeveland St A1
College Baths
Road C3
College Rd C2
Colletts Dr A1
Corpus St C3
Devonshire St A2
Douro Rd B1
Duke St B2
Dunalley Pde A2
Dunalley St A2

Everyman ▨ B2
Evesham Rd A3
Fairview Rd B3
Fairview St. B3
Fire Station C3
Folly La. A2
Gloucester Rd A1
Grosvenor St. B3
Grove St A1
Hanover St. A2
Hatherley St C1
Henrietta St. A2
Hewlett Rd. B3
High St B2/B3
Holst Birthplace
Museum ⌂ A3
Hudson St A2
Imperial Gdns C2
Imperial La B2
Imperial Sq. C2
Keynsham Rd C3
King St A2
Knapp Rd B2
Lansdown Cr C1
Lansdown Rd C1
Leighton Rd. B3
Library B2
London Rd C3
Lypiatt Rd C1
Magistrates' Court
& Register Office . . B1
Malvern Rd B1
Manser St. A1
Market St. A1
Marle Hill Pde A2
Marle Hill Rd. A2
Millbrook St A1
Milsom St A2
Montpellier Gdns . . . C2
Montpellier Grove . . C2
Montpellier Pde C2
Montpellier Spa Rd C2
Montpellier St. C1
Montpellier Terr. . . C2
Montpellier Walk . . C2

New St B2
North Pl B2
Old Bath Rd C3
Oriel Rd B2
Overton Park Rd . . . B1
Overton Rd B1
Oxford St C3
Parabola Rd. B1
Park Pl C1
Park St A1
Pittville Circus A3
Pittville Crescent . . A3
Pittville Lawn A3
Pittville Park A2
Playhouse ▨ B2
Portland St B3
Prestbury Rd A3
Prince's Rd C1
Priory St. B3
Promenade B2
Queen St A1
Recreation
Ground A2
Regent Arcade B2
Regent St B2
Rodney Rd B2
Royal Cr B2
Royal Well Pl B2
St George's Pl B1
St Georges Rd B1
St Gregory's ♠ B2
St James St B3
St John's Ave. B3
St Luke's Rd C2
St Margarets Rd . . . A2
St Mary's ♠ B2
St Matthew's ♠ . . . B2
St Paul's La A2
St Paul's Rd A2
St Paul's St. A2
St Stephen's Rd. . . . C1
Sandford Parks
Lido C3
Sandford Mill Rd. . . C3

Sandford Park C3
Sandford Rd C2
Selkirk St A3
Sherborne Pl. B3
Sherborne St. B3
Suffolk Pde C2
Suffolk Rd C1
Suffolk Sq C1
Sun St A2
Swindon Rd B2
Sydenham
Villas Rd C3
Tewkesbury Rd. A1
The Courtyard. B1
Thirlstaine Rd C2
Tivoli La C1
Tivoli St C1
Town Hall &
Theatre ▨ B2
Townsend St A1
Trafalgar St C2
Union St B3
University of
Gloucestershire
(Francis Close
Hall) A2
University of
Gloucestershire
(Hardwick) A1
Victoria Pl B3
Victoria St C2
Vittoria Walk C2
Wellesley Rd A2
Wellington Rd A3
Wellington Sq A3
Wellington St A2
West Drive A3
Western Rd B1
Wilson, The ⌂ B2
Winchcombe St B3
Winston Churchill
Memorial
Gardens ❀ A1

Chester

Abbey Gateway A2
Appleyards La C3
Bars, The B3
Bedward Row B1
Beeston View C3
Bishop Lloyd's
Palace ⌂ B2
Black Diamond St. . . A2
Bottoms La C3
Boughton. B3
Bouverie St A1
Bridge St B2
Bridgegate C2
Brook St A3
Brown's La C3
Cambrian Rd A1
Canal St A2
Carrick Rd C1
Castle ▥ C2
Castle Dr C2
Cathedral † B2
Catherine St A1
Cheshire Military
Museum ⌂ C2
Chester ≹ A3
Cheyney Rd A1
Chichester St A1
City Rd A3
City Walls B1/B2
City Walls Rd B1
Cornwall St A2
Cross Hey. C3
Cross, The ✦ B2
Crown Ct C2
Cuppin St B2
Curzon Park North . C1
Curzon Park South. . C1

Dee Basin. A1
Dee La. B3
Delamere St A2
Deva Roman
Discovery
Centre ⌂ B2
Dingle, The C1
Duke St. B2
Eastgate. B2
Eastgate St B2
Eaton Rd. C2
Edinburgh Way C3
Elizabeth Cr. B3
Fire Station A2
Foregate St B2
Forum Studio ▨ . . . B2
Forum, The B2
Frodsham St B2
Gamul House. B2
Garden La A1
George St A2
Gladstone Ave. A1
God's Providence
House ⌂ B2
Gorse Stacks A2
Greenway St C2
Grosvenor Bridge. . . C1
Grosvenor
Museum ⌂ B2
Grosvenor Park B3
Grosvenor Park
Terr. C1
Grosvenor
Shopping Ctr. B2
Grosvenor St. B2
Groves Rd B3
Groves, The B3
Guildhall
Museum ⌂ B1
Handbridge. C2

Hartington St C3
Hoole Way A2
Hunter St B2
Information Ctr ⌖ . . R2
King Charles'
Tower ✦ A2
King St A2
Library B2
Lightfoot St A3
Little Roodee C2
Liverpool Rd A2
Love St B3
Lower Bridge St . . . B2
Lower Park Rd. B3
Lyon St A2
Magistrates Court . . B2
Meadows La C3
Meadows, The C3
Milton St A3
Minerva Roman
Shrine ✦ C2
Miniature
Railway ✦ B3
New Crane St. B1
Nicholas St B2
Northgate A2
Northgate Arena . . . A2
Northgate St A2
Nun's Rd B1
Old Dee Bridge ✦ . . C2
Overleigh Rd C1
Park St B2
Police Station B2
Post Office ⌖ A2/A3
Princess St B2
Queen St B2
Queen's Park Rd . . . C3
Queen's Rd A3
Race Course B1
Raymond St A1

River La C2
Roman Amphitheatre
& Gardens ✦ B2
Roodee (Chester
Racecourse),
The B1
Russell St A3
St Anne St A2
St George's Cr C3
St Martin's Gate . . . A1
St Martin's Way. . . . B1
St Oswalds Way . . . A2
Saughall Rd A1
Sealand Rd A1
South View Rd. A1
Stanley Palace ⌂ . . . B1
Station Rd A3
Steven St A3
Storyhouse ▨ B2
Superstore B2
Tower Rd B1
Town Hall B2
Union St B3
University of
Chester C2
Vicar's La. B2
Victoria Cr. C3
Victoria Rd. A3
Walpole St. A1
Water Tower St A1
Water Tower,
The ✦ B1
Watergate B1
Watergate St. B2
Whipcord La A1
White Friars B2
York St B3

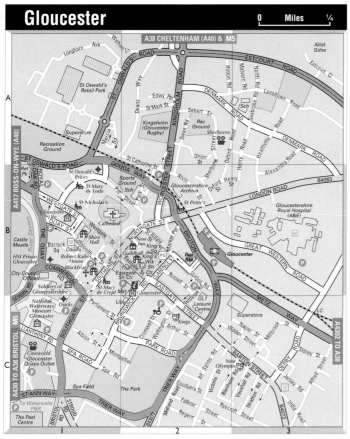

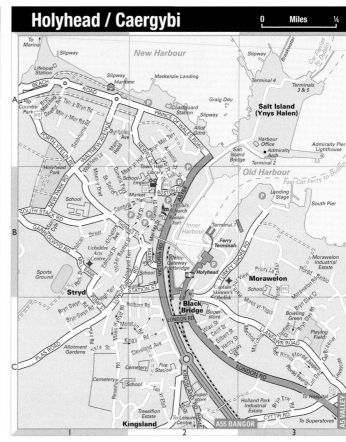

Gloucester

Albion St	.........C1	
Alexandra Rd	.....B3	
Alfred St	.........C3	
All Saints Rd	.....C2	
Alvin St	.........B2	
Arthur St	.........C2	
Barrack Square	...B1	
Barton St	.........C2	
Blackfriars †	......B1	
Blenheim Rd	......C2	
Bristol Rd	.........C1	
Brunswick Rd	.....C2	
Bruton Way	......B2	
Bus Station	......B2	
Cineworld 😎	....C1	
City Council		
Offices	.........B1	
Clarence St	......B2	
Commercial Rd	...B1	
Courts	...........B1	
Cromwell St	......C2	
Deans Way	......A2	
Denmark Rd	.....A3	
Derby Rd	.........C3	
Docks ✦	.........C1	
Eastgate St	......B2	
Eastgate, The	...B2	
Edwy Pde	.........A2	
Estcourt Cl	......A3	
Estcourt Rd	......A3	
Falkner St	.........C2	
GL1 Leisure		
Centre	.........C2	
Gloucester		
Cathedral †	......B1	
Gloucester Life 🏛	.B1	
Gloucester Quays		
Outlet	...........C1	

Gloucester Mus 🏛 .B2	
Gloucester		
Station ⟴	.......B2	
Gloucestershire		
Archive	......B2	
Gloucestershire		
Royal Hospital		
(A&E) Ⓗ	.......B3	
Goodyere St	......C2	
Gouda Way	......A1	
Great Western Rd . .B3	
Guildhall 🏛	.......B2	
Heathville Rd	....A3	
Henry Rd	.........B3	
Henry St	.........A2	
Hinton Rd	......A2	
HM Prison		
Gloucester ✦	....B1	
India Rd	.........C3	
Information Ctr 🅙 . .B2	
Jersey Rd	.........C3	
King's 🔱	.........C2	
King's Walk		
Shopping Centre . B2	
Kingsholm		
(Gloucester		
Rugby)	.........A2	
Kingsholm Rd	....A2	
Lansdown Rd	.....A3	
Library	...........C2	
Llanthony Rd	.....C1	
London Rd	......B3	
Longhorn Ave	....A1	
Longsmith St	.....B1	
Malvern Rd	......A3	
Market	...........B2	
Market Pde	......B2	
Mercia Rd	.........A1	
Metz Way	.........C2	
Midland Rd	.......C2	

Millbrook St	......C3	
Montpellier	.......C1	
Napier St	.........C3	
National Waterways		
Museum		
Gloucester 🏛	....C1	
Nettleton Rd	......C2	
New Inn 🏨	........B2	
New Olympus 🎭	...C3	
North Rd	.........A3	
Northgate St	.....B2	
Oxford Rd	.........A2	
Oxford St	.........B2	
Park & Ride		
Gloucester	......A1	
Park Rd	...........C1	
Park St	...........B2	
Park, The	.........C2	
Parliament St	.....C1	
Peel Centre, The . .C1	
Pitt St	...........B1	
Police Station		
🛡	.........B1/C3	
Post Office 📮	.....B2	
Quay St	...........B1	
Quay, The	.........B1	
Recreation Gd	.A1/A2	
Regent St	.........C2	
Robert Raikes		
House 🏠	.........B1	
Royal Oak Rd	.....B1	
Russell St	.........B2	
Ryecroft St	.........C2	
St Aldate St	.......B2	
St Ann Way	......C1	
St Catherine St	....A2	
St Mark St	.........A2	
St Mary de Crypt 🏛 .B1	
St Mary de Lode 🏛 . .B1	
St Nicholas's 🏛	.....B1	

St Oswald's		
Priory ✦	.........B1	
St Oswald's Rd	...A1	
St Oswald's		
Retail Park	......A1	
St Peter's 🏛	.......B2	
Seabroke Rd	......A3	
Sebert St	.........A2	
Severn Rd	.........C1	
Sherborne		
Cinema 😎	......B2	
Sherborne St	.....B2	
Shire Hall 🏛	......B1	
Sidney St	.........C3	
Soldiers of		
Gloucestershire		
🏛	.............B1	
Southgate St	.B1/C1	
Spa Field	.........C1	
Spa Rd	...........C1	
Sports Ground . A2/B2	
Station Rd	.........B2	
Stratton Rd	......C3	
Stroud Rd	.........C1	
Superstore	.......A1	
Swan Rd	.........A2	
Trier Way	.....C1/C2	
Union St	.........A2	
Vauxhall Rd	......C2	
Victoria St	.........C2	
Walham Lane	....A1	
Wellington St	.....C2	
Westgate Retail		
Park	...........B1	
Westgate St	.......B1	
Widden St	.........C2	
Worcester St	......B2	

Holyhead
Caergybi

Armenia St	.........A2	
Arthur St	.........C2	
Beach Rd	.........A1	
Boston St	.........B2	
Bowling Green	....C3	
Bryn Erw Rd	......C3	
Bryn Glas Cl	.......C3	
Bryn Glas Rd	......C3	
Bryn Gwyn Rd	....C3	
Bryn Marchog	....A1	
Bryn Mor Terr	....A2	
Bryngoleu Ave	...A3	
Cae Braenar	......C3	
Cambria St	.........A2	
Captain Skinner's		
Obelisk ✦	.......B2	
Cecil St	...........C2	
Celtic Gateway		
Footbridge	......B2	
Cemetery	.....C1/C2	
Cleveland Ave	....C2	
Coastguard		
Lookout	.........A2	
Court	.............A2	
Cybi Pl	...........A2	
Cyttir Rd	.........C3	
Edmund St	......B1	
Empire 😎	.........B2	
Ferry Terminals	...B2	

Ffordd Beibio	....B3	
Ffordd Feurig	.....C3	
Ffordd Hirnos	....C3	
Ffordd Jasper	.....C3	
Ffordd Tudur	.....B3	
Fire Station	......C2	
Garreglwyd Rd	...B1	
Gilbert St	.........C2	
Gorsedd Circle	...B1	
Gwelfor Ave	......A1	
Harbour Office	...A3	
Harbour View	....B3	
Henry St	.........C2	
High Terr	.........C1	
Hill St	...........B2	
Holborn Rd	......C3	
Holland Park		
Industrial Estate . .C3	
Holyhead Park	....B1	
Holyhead		
Station ⟴	.......B2	
King's Rd	.........C2	
Kingsland Rd	.....C2	
Lewascote	.......C3	
Library	...........B2	
Lifeboat Station	...A1	
Llanfawr Cl	.......C3	
Llanfawr Rd	......C3	
Lligwy St	.........C2	
Lon Deg	.........C3	
London Rd	......C3	
Longford Rd	.....B1	

Longford Terr	.....B1	
Maes Cybi	.........B1	
Maes Hedd	......A1	
Maes-Hyfryd Rd	...C1	
Maes-y-Dref	.....B1	
Maes-yr-Haf	.A2/B1	
Maes-yr-Ysgol	...C3	
Marchog	.........C3	
Marina	...........A1	
Maritime		
Museum 🏛	......A2	
Market	...........B2	
Market St	.........B2	
Mill Bank	.........B2	
Min-y-Mor Rd	....A1	
Morawelon		
Industrial Estate. .B3	
Morawelon Rd	....B3	
Moreton Rd	......C1	
New Park Rd	.....B1	
Newry St	.........A2	
Old Harbour		
Lighthouse	....A3	
Plas Rd	...........C1	
Police Station 🛡 . .B2	
Porth-y-Felin Rd . .A1	
Post Office		
📮	.......A1/B2/B3	
Prince of Wales Rd . A2	
Priory La	.........B3	
Pump St	.........C1	
Queens Park	.....B1	

Reseifion Rd	......C1	
Rock St	...........B1	
Roman Fort 🏛	....B2	
St Cybi St	.........B2	
St Cybi's Church 🏛 . B1	
St Seiriol's Cl	......B1	
Salt Island Bridge. . A2	
Seabourne Rd	....A1	
South Stack Rd	...B1	
Sports Ground	....B1	
Stanley St	.........B2	
Station St	.........B2	
Superstore	.......C2	
Tan-y-Bryn Rd	....A1	
Tan-yr-Efail	.......C3	
Tara St	...........C1	
Thomas St	.........B1	
Town Hall	.........A2	
Treseifion Estate . . C2	
Turkey Shore Rd . . B2	
Ucheldre		
Arts Centre ✦	....B1	
Ucheldre Ave	.....B1	
Upper Baptist St . . B1	
Victoria Rd	.........B2	
Victoria Terr	.......B1	
Vulcan St	.........C2	
Walthew Ave	.....A1	
Walthew La	.......A1	
Wian St	...........C2	

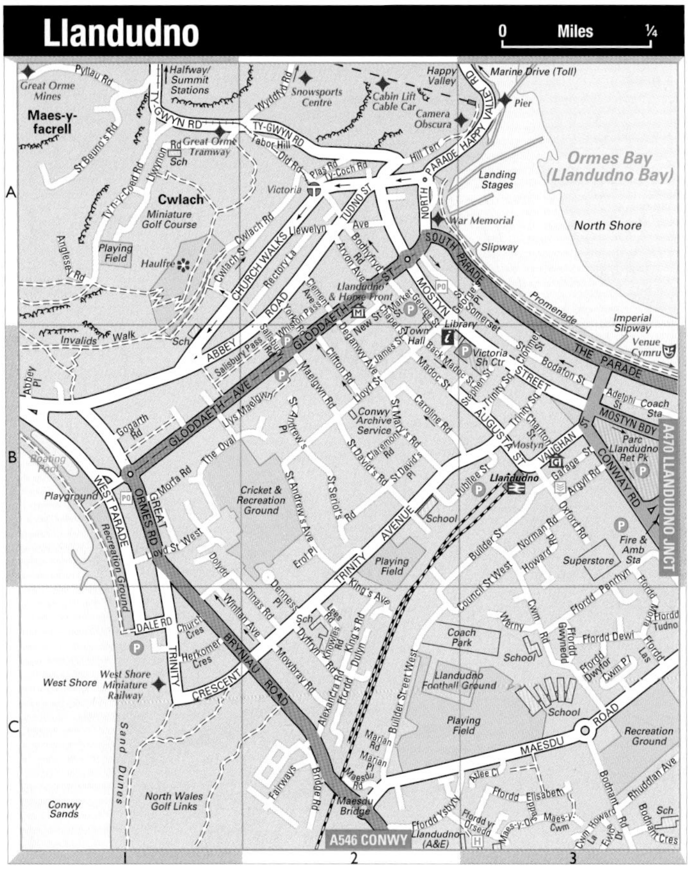

Llandudno
0 Miles ¼
Great Orme Mines
Maes-y-facrell
Halfway/Summit Stations
Snowsports Centre
Happy Valley
Cabin Lift Cable Car
Camera Obscura
Marine Drive (Toll)
Pier
Great Orme Tramway
Cwlach
Miniature Golf Course
Playing Field
Haulfre
Victoria
Landing Stages
Ormes Bay (Llandudno Bay)
North Shore
War Memorial
Slipway
Llandudno Home Front
Library
Town Hall
Victoria Sh Ctr
Promenade
Imperial Slipway
Venue Cymru
THE PARADE
Conwy Archive Service
Cricket & Recreation Ground
Parc Llandudno Ret Pk
Llandudno
School
Playing Field
Superstore
Fire & Amb Sta
A470 LLANDUDNO JNCT
Coach Park
Llandudno Football Ground
Playing Field
School
Recreation Ground
West Shore
West Shore Miniature Railway
Sand Dunes
North Wales Golf Links
Conwy Sands
Maesdu Bridge
Llandudno (A&E)
A546 CONWY
A
B
C
1
2
3

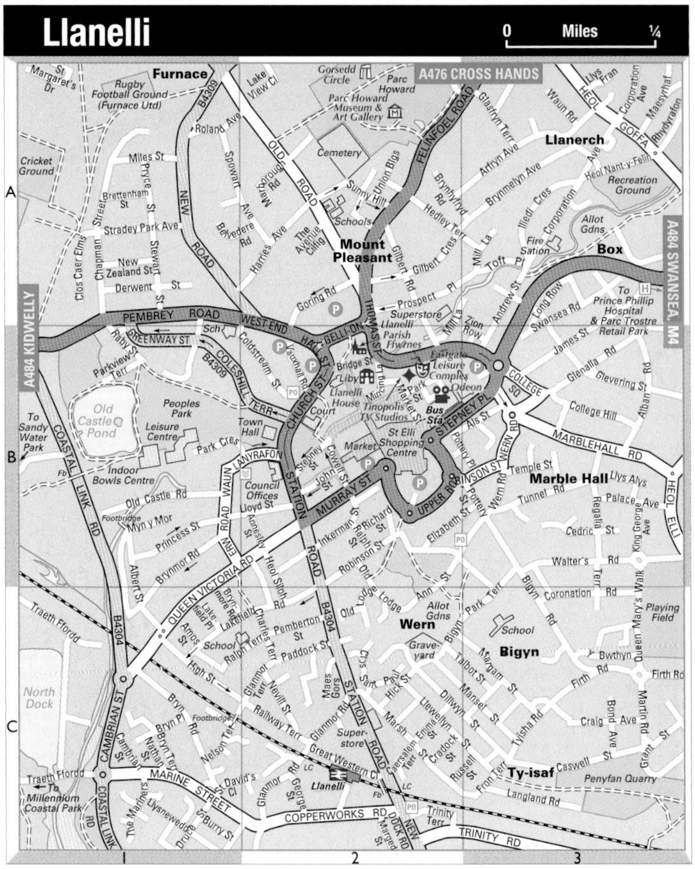

Llanelli
0 Miles ¼
Furnace
Rugby Football Ground (Furnace Utd)
Gorsedd Circle
Parc Howard
Parc Howard Museum & Art Gallery
A476 CROSS HANDS
Llanerch
Cricket Ground
Cemetery
Recreation Ground
Schools
Mount Pleasant
Allot Gdns
Fire Sation
Box
A484 SWANSEA, M4
A484 KIDWELLY
To Prince Phillip Hospital & Parc Trostre Retail Park
Superstore
Llanelli Parish Church
Eastgate Leisure Complex
Odeon
Llanelli House
Tinopolis TV Studios
Bus Sta
St Elli Shopping Centre
Market
Old Castle Pond
Peoples Park
Leisure Centre
Town Hall
To Sandy Water Park
Indoor Bowls Centre
Council Offices
Marble Hall
Playing Field
Wern
Allot Gdns
School
Grave-yard
Bigyn
North Dock
School
Super-store
Llanelli
Ty-isaf
Penyfan Quarry
Traeth Ffordd
Millennium Coastal Park
A
B
C
1
2
3

Llandudno

Abbey Pl . . . B1
Abbey Rd . . . B1
Adelphi St . . . B3
Alexandra Rd . . . C2
Anglesey Rd . . . A1
Argyll Rd . . . B3
Arvon Ave . . . A2
Atlee Cl . . . C3
Augusta St . . . B3
Back Madoc St . . . B2
Bodafon St . . . B3
Bodhyfryd Rd . . . A2
Bodnant Cr . . . C3
Bodnant Rd . . . C3
Bridge Rd . . . C2
Bryniau Rd . . . C1
Builder St . . . B3
Builder St West . . . C2
Cabin Lift Cable Car ✦ . . . A2
Camera Obscura ✦ A3
Caroline Rd . . . B2
Chapel St . . . A2
Charlton St . . . B3
Church Cr . . . C1
Church Walks . . . A2
Claremont Rd . . . B2
Clement Ave . . . A2
Clifton Rd . . . B2
Clonmel St . . . B3
Coach Station . . . B3
Conway Rd . . . B3
Conwy Archive Service . . . B2
Council St West . . . C3
Cricket and Recreation Ground . . . B2
Cwlach Rd . . . A2
Cwlach St . . . A1
Cwm Howard La . . . C3
Cwm Pl . . . C3
Cwm Rd . . . C3
Dale Rd . . . C1
Deganwy Ave . . . B2
Denness Pl . . . C2
Dinas Rd . . . C2
Dolydd . . . B1
Erol Pl . . . B2
Ewloe Dr . . . C3
Fairways . . . C2
Ffordd Dewi . . . C3
Ffordd Dulyn . . . C2
Ffordd Dwyfor . . . C3
Ffordd Elisabeth . . . C3
Ffordd Gwynedd . . . C3
Ffordd Las . . . C3
Ffordd Morfa . . . C3
Ffordd Penrhyn . . . C3
Ffordd Tudno . . . C3
Ffordd Ysbyty . . . C2
Fire & Ambulance Station . . . B3
Garage St . . . B3
George St . . . A2
Gloddaeth Ave . . . B1
Gloddaeth St . . . B2
Gogarth Rd . . . B1
Great Orme Mines ✦ . . . A1
Great Ormes Rd . . . B1
Great Orme Tramway ✦ . . . A2
Happy Valley . . . A2
Happy Valley Rd . . . A3
Haulfre Gardens ✿ A1
Herkomer Cr . . . C1
Hill Terr . . . A2
Home Front Museum 🏛 . . . B2
Hospice . . . B1
Howard Rd . . . B3
Information Ctr i . B2
Invalids' Walk . . . B1
James St . . . B2
Jubilee St . . . B3
King's Ave . . . C2
King's Rd . . . C2
Knowles Rd . . . C2
Lees Rd . . . C2
Library . . . B2
Llandudno 🏛 . . . A2
Llandudno (A&E) H C2
Llandudno Station ⇌ . . . B3
Llandudno Football Ground . . . C2
Llewelyn Ave . . . A2
Lloyd St . . . B2
Lloyd St West . . . B1
Llwynon Rd . . . A1
Llys Maelgwn . . . B1
Madoc St . . . B2
Maelgwn Rd . . . B2
Maes-y-Cwm . . . C3
Maes-y-Orsedd . . . C3
Maesdu Bridge . . . C2
Maesdu Rd . . . C2/C3
Marian Pl . . . C2
Marian Rd . . . C2
Marine Drive (Toll) . A3
Market St . . . A2
Miniature Golf Course . . . A1
Morfa Rd . . . B1
Mostyn 🏛 . . . B3
Mostyn Broadway . B3
Mostyn St . . . B3
Mowbray Rd . . . C2
New St . . . A2
Norman Rd . . . B3
North Parade . . . A2
North Wales Golf Links . . . C1
Old Bank, The 🏛 . . A2
Old Rd . . . A2
Oval, The . . . B1
Oxford Rd . . . B3
Parade, The . . . B3
Parc Llandudno Retail Park . . . B3
Pier ✦ . . . A3
Plas Rd . . . A2
Police Station ☒ . . . B3
Post Office PO . . A2/B3
Promenade . . . A3
Pyllau Rd . . . A1
Rectory La . . . A2
Rhuddlan Ave . . . C3
St Andrew's Ave . . . B2
St Andrew's Pl . . . B2
St Beuno's Rd . . . A1
St David's Pl . . . B2
St David's Rd . . . B2
St George's Pl . . . A3
St Mary's Rd . . . B2
St Seriol's Rd . . . B2
Salisbury Pass . . . B1
Salisbury Rd . . . B2
Somerset St . . . B3
South Parade . . . A2
Stephen St . . . B3
Tabor Hill . . . A2
Town Hall . . . B2
Trinity Ave . . . B1
Trinity Cres . . . C1
Trinity Sq . . . B3
Tudno St . . . A2
Ty-Coch Rd . . . A2
Ty-Gwyn Rd . . . A1/A2
Ty'n-y-Coed Rd . . . A1
Vaughan St . . . B3
Victoria Shopping Centre . . . B3
Victoria 🚡 . . . A2
War Memorial ✦ . . A2
Werny Wylan . . . C3
West Parade . . . B1
Whiston Pass . . . A2
Winllan Ave . . . C2
Wyddfyd Rd . . . A2
York Rd . . . A2

Llanelli

Alban Rd . . . B3
Albert St . . . B1
Als St . . . B3
Amos St . . . C1
Andrew St . . . A3
Ann St . . . C2
Annesley St . . . B2
Arfryn Ave . . . A3
Avenue Cilfig, The . A2
Belvedere Rd . . . A1
Bigyn Park Terr . . . C3
Bigyn Rd . . . C3
Bond Ave . . . C3
Brettenham St . . . A1
Bridge St . . . B2
Bryn Pl . . . C1
Bryn Rd . . . C1
Bryn Terr . . . C1
Bryn-More Rd . . . C1
Brynhyfryd Rd . . . A2
Brynmelyn Ave . . . A3
Brynmor Rd . . . B1
Burry St . . . C1
Bus Station . . . B2
Caersalem Terr . . . C2
Cambrian St . . . C1
Caswell St . . . C3
Cedric St . . . B3
Cemetery . . . A2
Chapman St . . . A1
Charles Terr . . . C2
Church St . . . B2
Clos Caer Elms . . . A1
Clos Sant Paul . . . C2
Coastal Link Rd . B1/C1
Coldstream St . . . B2
Coleshill Terr . . . B1
College Hill . . . B3
College Sq . . . B3
Copperworks Rd . . C2
Coronation Rd . . . C3
Corporation Ave . . A3
Council Offices . . . B2
Court . . . B2
Cowell St . . . B2
Cradock St . . . C2
Craig Ave . . . C3
Cricket Ground . . . A1
Derwent St . . . A1
Dillwyn St . . . C2
Druce St . . . C1
Eastgate Leisure Complex ✦ . . . B2
Elizabeth St . . . B2
Emma St . . . C2
Erw Rd . . . B1
Felinfoel Rd . . . A2
Fire Station . . . A3
Firth Rd . . . C3
Fron Terr . . . C3
Furnace United Rugby Football Ground . . . A1
Gelli-On . . . B2
George St . . . C2
Gilbert Cres . . . A2
Gilbert Rd . . . A2
Glanmor Rd . . . C2
Glanmor Terr . . . C2
Glasfryn Terr . . . A3
Glenalla Rd . . . B3
Glevering St . . . B3
Goring Rd . . . A2
Gorsedd Circle ⛩ . . A2
Grant St . . . C3
Graveyard . . . C3
Great Western Cl . . C2
Greenway St . . . B1
Hall St . . . B2
Harries Ave . . . A2
Hedley Terr . . . A2
Heol Elli . . . B3
Heol Goffa . . . A3
Heol Nant-y-Felin . A3
Heol Siloh . . . B2
Hick St . . . C2
High St . . . C1
Indoor Bowls Centre . . . B1
Inkerman St . . . B2
Island Pl . . . B2
James St . . . B3
John St . . . B2
King George Ave . . B3
Lake View Cl . . . A2
Lakefield Pl . . . C1
Lakefield Rd . . . C1
Langland Rd . . . C3
Leisure Centre . . . B1
Library . . . B2
Llanelli House 🏛 . . . B2
Llanelli Parish Church ⛪ . . . B2
Llanelli Station ⇌ . C2
Llewellyn St . . . C2
Lliedi Cres . . . A3
Lloyd St . . . B2
Llys Alys . . . B3
Llys Fran . . . A3
Llysnewedd . . . C1
Long Row . . . A3
Maes Gors . . . C2
Maesyrhaf . . . A3
Mansel St . . . C3
Marblehall Rd . . . B3
Marborough Rd . . A2
Margam St . . . C3
Marged St . . . C2
Marine St . . . C1
Mariners, The . . . C1
Market . . . B2
Market St . . . B2
Marsh St . . . C2
Martin Rd . . . C3
Miles St . . . A1
Mill La . . . A3/B2
Mincing La . . . B2
Murray St . . . B2
Myn y Mor . . . B1
Nathan St . . . C1
Nelson Terr . . . C1
Nevill St . . . C2
New Dock Rd . . . C2
New Rd . . . A1
New Zealand St . . . A1
Odeon 🎥 . . . B2
Old Lodge . . . C2
Old Rd . . . A2
Paddock St . . . C2
Palace Ave . . . B3
Parc Howard . . . A2
Parc Howard Museum & Art Gallery 🏛 A2
Park Cres . . . B1
Park St . . . B2
Parkview Terr . . . B1
Pemberton St . . . C2
Pembrey Rd . . . A1
Peoples Park . . . B1
Police Station ☒ . . B2
Post Office PO . . B2/C2
Pottery Pl . . . B3
Pottery St . . . B3
Princess St . . . B1
Prospect Pl . . . A2
Pryce St . . . A1
Queen Mary's Walk C3
Queen Victoria Rd . C1
Raby St . . . B1
Railway Terr . . . C2
Ralph St . . . B2
Ralph Terr . . . C1
Regalia Terr . . . B3
Rhydyrafon . . . A3
Richard St . . . B2
Robinson St . . . B2
Roland Ave . . . A1
Russell St . . . C3
St David's Cl . . . C1
St Elli Shopping Centre . . . B2
St Margaret's Dr . . A1
Spowart Ave . . . A1
Station Rd . . . B2/C2
Stepney Pl . . . B2
Stepney St . . . B2
Stewart St . . . A1
Stradey Park Ave . . A1
Sunny Hill . . . A2
Superstore . . . A2
Swansea Rd . . . A3
Talbot St . . . C3
Temple St . . . B3
Thomas St . . . A2
Tinopolos TV Studios ✦ . . . B2
Toft Pl . . . A3
Town Hall . . . B2
Traeth Ffordd . . . C1
Trinity Rd . . . C3
Trinity Terr . . . C2
Tunnel Rd . . . B3
Tyisha Rd . . . C3
Union Blgs . . . A2
Upper Robinson St . B2
Vauxhall Rd . . . B2
Walter's Rd . . . B3
Waun Lanyrafon . . . B2
Waun Rd . . . A3
Wern Rd . . . B3
West End . . . A2
Y Bwthyn . . . C3
Zion Row . . . B3

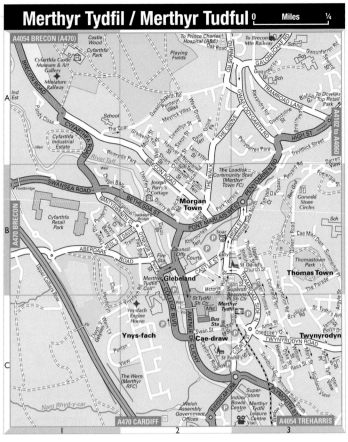

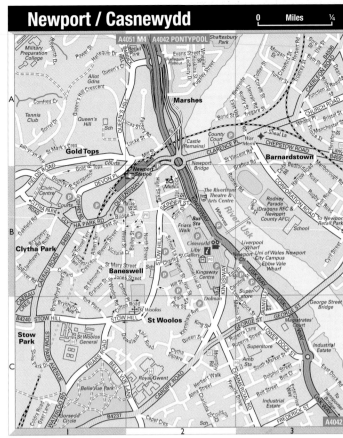

Merthyr Tydfil
Merthyr Tudful

Aberdare Rd B2
Abermorlais Terr . . B2
Alexandra Rd A3
Alma St. C3
Arfryn Pl. C3
Argyle St C3
Avenue De Clichy . . C2
Beacons Place
　Shopping Centre . C2
Bethesda St. B2
Bishops Grove. . . . A3
Brecon Rd A1/B2
Briarmead A3
Bryn St C3
Bryntirion Rd. . . B3/C3
Bus Station B2
Cae Mari Dwn B3
Caedraw Rd C2
Castle Sq A1
Castle St. B2
Chapel C2
Chapel Bank B1
Church St. B3
Civic Centre. B2
Clos Penderyn B1
Coedcae'r Ct C3
College
　Boulevard C2
County and
　Crown Courts C2
Court St C3
Cromwell St. B2
Cyfarthfa Castle,
　Museum and
　Art Gallery ⌂ A1
Cyfarthfa
　Industrial Estate. . A1
Cyfarthfa Park A1
Cyfarthfa
　Retail Park. B1
Cyfarthfa Rd A1

Dane St. A2
Dane Terr. A2
Danyparc. B3
Darren View A3
Dixon St B2
Dyke St C3
Dynevor St. C3
Elwyn Dr. C3
Fire Station B2
Fothergill St B2
Galonuchaf Rd A3
Garth St B2
Georgetown B2
Grawen Terr A2
Grove Pk. A2
Grove, The A2
Gurnos Rd A2
Gwaelodygarth
　Rd A2/A3
Gwaunfarren Grove A3
Gwaunfarren Rd. . . A3
Gwendoline St A3
Hampton St C3
Hanover St. C3
Heol S O Davies. . . B1
Heol-Gerrig B1
High St . . A3/B2/B3/C2
Highland View. . . . B3
Howell Cl B1
Jackson's Bridge . . B2
James St B3
John St B3
Joseph Parry's
　Cottage ⌂ B2
Lancaster St A2
Library C2
Llewellyn St. A2
Llwyfen St B2
Llwyn Berry B1
Llwyn Dic
　Penderyn. B1
Llwyn-y-Gelynen. . . C1
Lower Thomas St . . B3
Market C2

Mary St C3
Masonic St. C2
Merthyr Tydfil
　College. B2
Merthyr Town FC . . B3
Merthyr Tydfil
　Leisure Centre . . C3
Merthyr Tydfil
　Station ₪ C3
Meyrick Villas A2
Miniature
　Railway ✦ A1
Mount St C3
Nantygwenith St. . . B1
Norman Terr B2
Oak Rd A2
Old Cemetery B3
Pandy Cl A2
Pantycelynen B1
Parade, The C3
Park Terr B2
Penlan View C2
Penry St C3
Pentwyn Villas . . . A2
Penyard Rd B2
Penydarren Park . . A3
Penydarren Rd B3
Plymouth St C3
Police Station ⍟. . . C2
Pont Marlais West . B2
Post Office ℗ B2
Quarry Row B2
Queen's Rd B3
Rees St C3
Rhydycar Link C2
Riverside Park A1
St David's ⛪. B3
St Tydfil's ⛪ C2
St Tydfil's Ave C2
St Tydfil's Square
　Shopping Centre . C2
Saxon St A2
School of Nursing . . A2
Seward St A3

Shiloh La B3
Stone Circles ⌂. . . . B3
Stuart St. A2
Summerhill Pl. B3
Superstore B3
Swan St C2
Swansea Rd B1
Taff Glen View. . . . C3
Taff Vale Ct C3
Theatre Soar ☺ . . . B2
Thomastown Park . B3
Tramroad La A3
Tramroad Side B2
Tramroad Side
　North B3
Tramroad Side
　South C3
Trevithick Gdns . . . C3
Trevithick St A3
Tudor Terr B2
Twynyrodyn Rd . . . C3
Union St B3
Upper Colliers
　Row. A2
Upper Thomas St . . B3
Victoria St B2
Vue 🎬. C3
Vulcan Rd. B2
Walk, The B2
Warlow St C3
Well St A2
Welsh Assembly
　Government
　Offices C2
Wern La C1
Wern, The
　(Merthyr RFC) . . . C2
West Grove A2
William St C3
Yew St. C3
Ynysfach Engine
　House ✦ C2
Ynysfach Rd. C2

Newport
Casnewydd

Albert Terr. B1
Allt-yr-Yn Ave. A1
Alma St. C2
Ambulance Sta A3
Bailey St. B2
Barrack Hill A2
Bath St A3
Bedford Rd B3
Belle Vue La. C1
Belle Vue Park. . . . C1
Bishop St A3
Blewitt St. B1
Bolt Cl. C3
Bolt St. C3
Bond St. B1
Bosworth Dr A1
Bridge St B1
Bristol St A3
Bryngwyn Rd. C1
Brynhyfryd Ave. . . . C1
Brynhyfryd Rd. C1
Bus Station B2
Caerau Cres. C1
Caerau Rd B1
Caerleon Rd. A3
Capel Cres. C2
Cardiff Rd C2
Caroline St. B3
Castle (Remains) . . A2
Cedar Rd B3
Charles St B1
Charlotte Dr C2
Chepstow Rd A3
Church Rd A3
Cineworld 🎬 B2
Civic Centre. B1
Clarence Pl A2
Clifton Pl B1
Clifton Rd. C1
Clyffard Cres. B1
Clytha Park Rd B1
Clytha Sq C2
Coldra Rd C1
Collier St A3
Colne St B3
Comfrey Cl. A1
Commercial Rd. . . . C3

Commercial St B2
Corelli St A3
Corn St. B2
Corporation Rd. . . . A3
Coulson Cl C2
County Court. A3
Courts A1/B1
Crawford St A3
Cyril St B3
Dean St. B1
Devon Pl. B1
Dewsland Park Rd . . C2
Dolman ☺ B2
Dolphin St C3
East Dock Rd C3
East St A3
East Usk Rd A3
Ebbw Vale Wharf . . B3
Emlyn St. B2
Enterprise Way. . . . C3
Eton Rd. B3
Evans St A2
Factory Rd A2
Fields Rd B1
Francis Dr C2
Frederick St C3
Friars Rd C1
Friars Walk B2
Gaer La C1
George St. C3
George Street
　Bridge C3
Godfrey Rd. B1
Gold Tops B1
Gore St A3
Gorsedd Circle C1
Grafton Rd A2
Graham St B1
Granville St C3
Harlequin Dr A1
Harrow Rd B3
Herbert Rd A3
Herbert Walk C2
Hereford St A3
High St B2
Hill St B2
Hoskins St A2
Information Ctr ℹ . . B2
Ivor St B2
Jones St B1

Junction Rd A3
Keynshaw Ave C2
King St C2
Kingsway. B2
Kingsway Centre . . B2
Ledbury Dr A2
Library A3
Library, Museum &
　Art Gallery ⌂ . . . B2
Liverpool Wharf . . . B3
Llanthewy Rd B1
Llanvair Rd. A3
Locke St A2
Lower Dock St. C3
Lucas St A2
Manchester St A3
Market B2
Marlborough Rd . . . B3
Mellon St C3
Military Preparation
　College. A1
Mill St A2
Morgan St A3
Mountjoy Rd C2
Newport Bridge . . . A2
Newport Ctr B2
Newport Station ₪ . B2
North St B2
Oakfield Rd B1
Park Sq. C2
Police
　Station ⍟. A3/C2
Post Office ℗ . . . B2/C3
Power St. A1
Prince St A3
Pugsley St A2
Queen St C2
Queen's Cl A1
Queen's Hill. A1
Queen's Hill Cres . . A1
Queensway B2
Railway St. B2
Riverfront Theatre &
　Arts Centre,
　The ☺ B2
Riverside A3
Rodney Parade
　(Dragons RFC &
　Newport County
　AFC) B3

Rodney Rd B2
Royal Gwent ⊞ C2
Rudry St A3
Rugby Rd B3
Ruperra La. C3
Ruperra St C3
St Edmund St B1
St Mary St B1
St Vincent Rd A3
St Woolos ✝. C2
St Woolos General
　(no A&E) C1
St Woolos Rd B1
School La B1
Serpentine Rd. B1
Shaftesbury Park . . A2
Sheaf La A3
Skinner St B2
Sorrel Dr A1
South Market St . . . C3
Spencer Rd B1
Stow Hill B2/C1/C2
Stow Park Ave C1
Stow Park Dr C1
Talbot St. B2
Tennis Club A1
Tregare St A3
Trostrey St A3
Tunnel Terr B1
Turner St A3
Univ of Wales
　Newport City
　Campus B3
Upper Dock St. B2
Usk St A3
Usk Way B3/C3
Exeter Cres B1
War Memorial A3
Waterloo Rd C1
West St. B1
Wharves. B2
Wheeler St. A2
Whitby Pl A3
Windsor Terr. B1
York Pl C1

Newtown / Y Drenewydd

0 Miles ¼

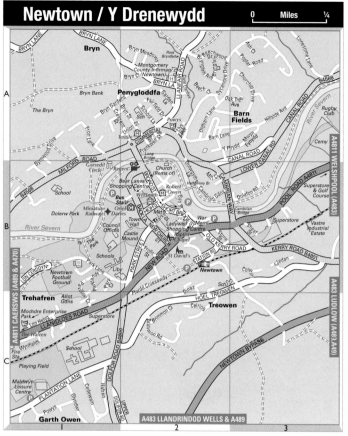

Shrewsbury

0 Miles ¼

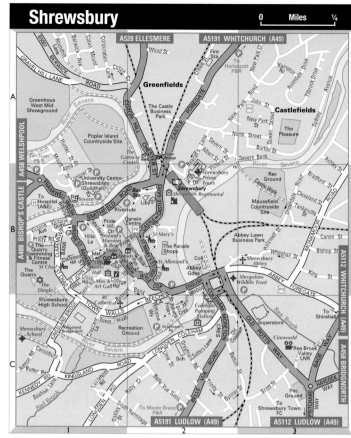

Swansea / Abertawe

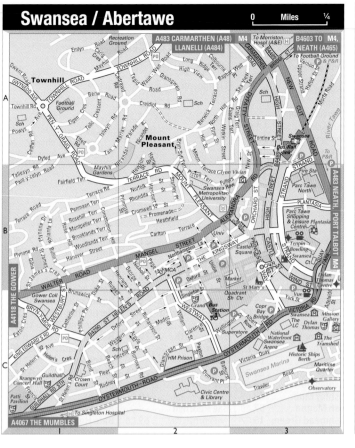

Wrexham / Wrecsam

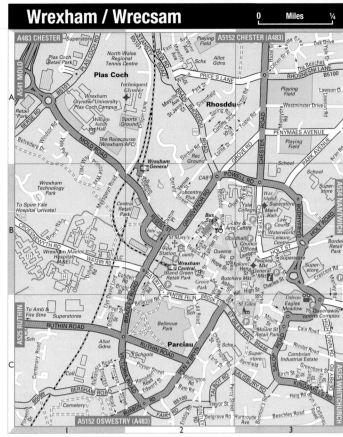

Swansea
Abertawe

Adelaide St C3
Albert Row. C3
Alexandra Rd. B2
Argyle St C1
Baptist Well Pl A2
Beach St C1
Belle Vue Way B3
Berw Rd A1
Berwick Terr C1
Bond St. C1
Brangwyn
  Concert Hall 🎭 . . .C1
Bridge St A3
Brooklands Terr B1
Brunswick St C1
Bryn-Syfi Terr A2
Bryn-y-Mor Rd C1
Bullins La C1
Burrows Rd B3
Bus Station C2
Bus/Rail link A3
Cadfan Rd A1
Cadrawd Rd A1
Caer St B3
Carig Cres A1
Carlton Terr. B2
Carmarthen Rd A3
Castle Square B3
Castle St. B3
Catherine St C1
Civic Centre &
  Library C2
Clarence St C2
Colbourne
  Terrace. A2
Constitution Hill. . . .B1
Copr Bay Bridge B3
Court B3
Creidiol Rd. A1
Cromwell St. B2
Crown Courts C1
Duke St C1
Dunvant Pl. C2
Dyfatty Park A3
Dyfatty St. A3
Dyfed Ave. A1
Dylan Thomas
  Ctr ✦ B3

Dylan Thomas
  Theatre 🎭 C3
Eaton Cres C1
Eigen Cres A1
Elfed Rd A1
Emlyn Rd A1
Evans Terr A3
Fairfield Terr. B1
Ffynone Dr. B1
Ffynone Rd B1
Fire Station B3
Firm St A2
Fleet St. C1
Francis St. C1
Fullers Row B2
George St. C1
Glamorgan St C2
Glynn Vivian
  Art Gall 🏛 B3
Gower Coll
  Swansea. C1
Graig Terr A3
Grand Theatre 🎭 . .C2
Granogwen Rd A2
Guildhall C1
Guildhall Rd South . .C1
Gwent Rd A1
Gwynedd Ave A1
Hafod St. A3
Hanover St. B1
Harcourt St B2
Harries St A2
Heathfield B2
Henrietta St B2
Hewson St B2
High St A3/B3
High View A2
Hill St A2
Historic Ships
  Berth ⚓ C3
HM Prison C2
Islwyn Rd A1
King Edward's Rd . . .B2
Kingsway, The B2
LC, The C3
Long Ridge A1
Madoc St C2
Mansel St B2
Maritime Quarter . . .C3
Market B3
Mayhill Gdns B1

Mayhill Rd A1
Milton Terr. A2
Mission Gallery 🏛 . .C3
Montpelier Terr B1
Morfa Rd A3
Mount Pleasant B2
National Waterfront
  Museum 🏛 C3
New Cut Rd A3
New St A3
Nicander Pde A2
Nicander Pl A2
Nicholl St B2
Norfolk St B2
North Hill Rd A2
Northampton La B2
Observatory ✦ C3
Odeon 🎬 C3
Orchard St B3
Oxford St B2
Oystermouth Rd C1
Page St B2
Pant-y-Celyn Rd. . . .B1
Parc Tawe North B3
Parc Tawe Shopping
  & Leisure Centre . .B3
Patti Pavilion 🎭 . . .C1
Paxton St C2
Pen-y-Graig Rd A1
Penmaen Terr. B1
Phillips Pde C1
Picton Terr B2
Plantasia B3
Plantasia 🌸 B3
Police Station 🏛. . . .B2
Post Office
  🏤 A1/A2/C1
Powys Ave A1
Primrose St B2
Princess Way. B3
Promenade B2
Pryder Gdns A2
Quadrant
  Shopping Ctr. C2
Quay Park B3
Rhianfa La B1
Rhondda St. B2
Richardson St C2
Rodney St C1
Rose Hill B1
Rosehill Terr B1

Russell St. B1
St Helen's Ave C1
St Helen's Cres C1
St Helen's Rd C1
St James Gdns B1
St James's Cres B1
St Mary's ⛪ B3
Sea View Terr A3
Singleton St C2
Stanley Pl. A3
Strand B3
Swansea Arena. C3
Swansea Castle 🏰 . .B3
Swansea
  Metropolitan
  University B2
Swansea
  Museum 🏛 C3
Swansea
  Station ⬛ A3
Taliesyn Rd A1
Tan y Marian Rd A1
Tegid Rd A2
Teilo Cres. A1
Tenpin Bowling ✦ . .B3
Terrace Rd B1/B2
Tontine St A3
Townhill Rd A1
Tramshed, The 🏛. . .C3
Trawler Rd C3
Union St B2
Upper Strand A3
Vernon St. C3
Victoria Quay C3
Victoria Rd. B3
Vincent St C1
Vue 🎬 C3
Walter Rd B1
Watkin St A2
Waun-Wen Rd A2
Wellington St C2
Westbury St. C1
Western St C1
Westway C2
William St C2
Wind St. B3
Woodlands Terr B1
YMCA B2
York St C3

Wrexham
Wrecsam

Abbot St B2
Acton Rd A3
Albert St. C3
Alexandra Rd. C1
Aran Rd A3
Barnfield C3
Bath Rd. C2
Beeches, The A3
Beechley Rd C3
Belgrave Rd. C2
Bellevue Park C2
Bellevue Rd. C2
Belvedere Dr. A1
Bennion's Rd C3
Berse Rd A1
Bersham Rd. C1
Birch St C3
Bodhyfryd B2
Border Retail Park . .B3
Bradley Rd C2
Bright St. B1
Bron-y-Nant B3
Brook St C2
Bryn-y-Cabanau
  Rd C3
Bury St C3
Bus Station B2
Butchers Market B2
Caia Rd C3
Cambrian Industrial
  Estate. C3
Caxton Pl B2
Cemetery C1
Centenary Rd C3
Central Retail Park. . .B2
Chapel St C2
Charles St B3
Chester Rd. A3
Chester St B3
Cilcen Grove A3
Citizens Advice
  Bureau B2
Cobden Rd. C3
Council Offices. B3
County B3
Crescent Rd. C3
Crispin La. A2
Croesnewyth Rd. . . .B1

Cross St A2
Cunliffe St A2
Derby Rd C3
Dolydd Rd B1
Duke St. B2
Eagles Meadow C3
Earle St. C2
East Ave A2
Edward St C2
Egerton St B2
Empress Rd C1
Erddig Rd C1
Fairy Rd C2
Fire Station B2
Foxwood Dr. C1
Garden Rd A2
General Market B3
Gerald St B2
Gibson St C1
Greenbank St C3
Greenfield A2
Grosvenor Rd B2
Grove Park 🎭 B2
Grove Park Rd B3
Grove Rd A3
Guildhall B2
Haig Rd. C3
Hampden Rd C3
Hazel Grove. A3
Henblas St B3
High St B2
Hightown Rd C3
Hill St B2
Holt Rd B3
Holt St C3
Hope St B2
Huntroyde Ave C3
Information
  Centre 🅹 B3
Island Green
  Retail Park. B2
Jobcentre Plus B2
Jubilee Rd C3
King St B3
Kingsmills Rd C3
Lambpit St. B3
Law Courts B3
Lawson Cl A3
Lawson Rd A3
Lea Rd. C2

Library &
  Arts Centre B2
Lilac Way B1
Llys David Lord B1
Lorne St A2
Maesgwyn Rd B1
Maesydre Rd A3
Manley Rd B3
Market St. B3
Mawddy Ave A2
Mayville Ave A2
Memorial Hall B3
Mold Rd A1
Mount St C3
Mount Street
  Retail Park. C3
Neville Cres A3
New Rd C2
North Wales Regional
  Tennis Centre A1
Oak Dr. C3
Odeon 🎬 C3
Park Ave. A3
Park St C2
Peel St C1
Pen y Bryn C2
Pentre Felin C2
Penymaes Ave. A3
Peoples Market B3
Percy St C2
Pines, The A3
Plas Coch Rd A1
Plas Coch
  Retail Park. A1
Poplar Rd C2
Post Office
  🏤 A2/B3/C3
Powell Rd. B3
Poyser St C3
Price's La. A2
Primose Way B1
Princess St C1
Queen St B3
Queens Sq B2
Regent St B3
Rhosddu Rd. A2/B2
Rhosnesni La. A3
Rivulet Rd C2
Ruabon Rd C2
Ruthin Rd C1/C2
St Giles ⛪ C3

St Giles Way. C3
St James Ct A2
St Mary's ✝ B2
Salisbury Rd C3
Salop Rd. C3
Sontley Rd C2
Spring Rd C3
Stanley St. C3
Stansty Rd A2
Station Approach. . . .B2
Superstore .A1/B3/C1
Talbot Rd C2
Techniquest
  Glyndwr ✦ A2
Town Hill C2
Trevor St C2
Trinity St B2
Tuttle St C2
Vale Park A1
Vernon St. B2
Vicarage Hill B2
Victoria Rd. A2
Walnut St A2
War Memorial ✦ B3
Waterworld Leisure
  Centre ✦ B3
Watery Rd B1/B2
Wellington Rd C2
Westminster Dr A3
William Aston
  Hall 🎭 A1
Windsor Rd A1
Wrecsam C3
Wrexham AFC A1
Wrexham
  Central ⬛ B2
Wrexham
  General ⬛ B2
Wrexham Glyndwr
  University Plas
  Coch Campus A1
Wrexham Maelor
  Hospital (A&E) 🏥 . .B1
Wrexham
  Technology Park . .B1
Wynn Ave A3
Xplore! ✦ B3
Yale College A3
Yale Grove A3
Yorke St C3

Index to road maps

Abbreviations used in the index

Anglesey **Isle of Anglesey**
Bath **Bath and North East Somerset**
Bl Gwent **Blaenau Gwent**
Bridgend **Bridgend**
Bristol **City and County of Bristol**
Caerph **Caerphilly**
Cardiff **Cardiff**
Carms **Carmarthenshire**
Ceredig **Ceredigion**
Ches **Cheshire**
Conwy **Conwy**

Denb **Denbighshire**
Flint **Flintshire**
Glos **Gloucesterhire**
Gtr Man **Greater Manchester**
Gwyn **Gwynedd**
Hereford **Herefordshire**
M Tydf **Merthyr Tydfil**
Mers **Merseyside**
Mon **Monmouthshire**
N Som **North Somerset**
Neath **Neath Port Talbot**
Newport **City and County of Newport**

Pembs **Pembrokeshire**
Powys **Powys**
Rhondda **Rhondda Cynon Taff**
S Glos **South Gloucestershire**
Shrops **Shropshire**
Som **Somerset**
Swansea **Swansea**
Torf **Torfaen**
V Glam **The Vale of Glamorgan**
Wilts **Wiltshire**
Wrex **Wrexham**

How to use the index

Example

Llangower Gwyn   54 B3

— grid square
— page number
— county or unitary authority

Abb–Ben

A

Abbey-cwm-hir . 41 D6
Abbeydale 29 D7
Abbey Dore 27 A5
Abbey Green 57 B7
Abbots Leigh 6 B2
Abbot's Meads . . . 72 F2
Abcott 43 C5
Aber 32 C2
Aberaeron 38 F2
Aberaman 11 B7
Aberangell 45 A7
Aber-Arad 31 E6
Aberarth 38 F2
Aber-banc 31 D7
Aberbargoed 12 B3
Aberbechan 47 E6
Aberbeeg 12 B4
Aberbran 24 B4
Abercanaid 11 B8
Abercarn 12 D4
Abercastle 18 C5
Abercegir 45 C7
Aber Cowarch . . . 54 E2
Abercraf 23 E9
Abercwmboi 11 C7
Abercych 30 D4
Abercynafon 25 D6
Abercynffig
= Aberkenfig 10 F4
Abercynon 11 C8
Aberdâr
= Aberdare 11 B6
Aberdare
= Aberdâr 11 B6
Aberdaron 50 C3
Aberdesach 58 D4
Aberdovey
= Aberdyfi 44 D3
Aberdulais 10 B2
Aberdyfi
= Aberdovey 44 D3
Aberedw 35 C6
Abereiddy 18 C3
Abererch 51 A7
Aberfan 11 B8
Aberffraw 66 F4
Aberffrwd 39 C6
Abergarw 11 F5
Abergarwed 10 B3
Abergavenny 26 E3
Abergele 69 D8
Aber-Giâr 32 D3
Abergorlech 22 A4
Abergwaun
= Fishguard 19 B7
Abergwesyn 34 B2
Abergwili 22 C1
Abergwynant 53 E5
Abergwyngregyn 68 E3
Abergynolwyn . . . 44 B4

Aber-Hirnant 54 B4
Aberhosan 45 D7
Aberkenfig
= Abercynffig 10 F4
Aberlerry 44 E3
Aberllefenni 45 B6
Aberllydan
= Broad Haven . . . 16 B3
Aberllynfi
= Three Cocks . . . 35 E8
Abermagwr 39 D6
Abermaw
= Barmouth 52 E4
Abermeurig 32 A4
Aber miwl
= Abermule 47 E7
Abermorddu 63 C7
Abermule
= Aber-miwl 47 E7
Abernaint 55 D7
Abernant 21 C6
Aber-nant 11 B7
Aber-oer 63 E6
Aberogwr
= Ogmore by Sea . 2 A4
Aberpennar
= Mountain Ash . . 11 C7
Aberporth 31 B5
Aber-Rhiwlech . . 54 D3
Aberriw
= Berriew 47 C7
Abersoch 51 C6
Abersychan 12 B5
Abertawe
= Swansea 9 D7
Aberteifi
= Cardigan 30 C3
Aberthin 3 A7
Abertillery 12 B4
Abertridwr 12 E2
Abertrinant 44 B3
Abertysswg 12 A2
Aber-Village 25 C7
Aberyscir 24 B4
Aberystwyth 38 B4
Abson 7 B6
Achddu 8 B3
Acrefair 63 F6
Acton Bridge . . . 73 D6
Acton Burnell . . . 49 C6
Acton Pigott 49 C6
Acton Reynald . . 57 D7
Acton Round 49 D8
Acton Turville . . . 15 F8
Adfa 46 C5
Adforton 43 D6
Adpar 31 D6
Afon Eitha 63 E6
Afon-wen 70 C4
Afon Wen 51 A8
Aifft 70 F4
Aigburth 72 B2
Ailey 36 C4
Aithnen 55 D9
Alberbury 56 F4

Albert Town 16 A4
Albro Castle 30 C3
Alcaston 49 F5
Alderley 15 D7
Aldersey Green . . 64 C2
Aldford 64 C1
Aldon 43 C6
Ale Oak 42 B2
Alkerton 15 A7
Alkington 57 A7
Allaston 14 B4
Allensmore 37 E7
Allerton 72 B3
All Stretton 49 D5
Allt 9 B6
Alltforgan 54 D4
Alltmawr 35 C6
Alltwalis 21 A8
Alltwen 10 B1
Alltyblaca 32 C3
Allt-yr-yn 13 E5
Almeley 36 B4
Almeley Wooton . 36 B4
Almondsbury . . . 14 F4
Alpraham 64 C4
Alsager 65 C8
Altbough 27 A8
Alvanley 72 E4
Alveston 14 E4
Alveston Down . . 14 E4
Alvington 14 B4
Alway 13 E6
Ambleston 19 D8
Amesbury 7 E5
Amlwch 67 A5
Amlwch Port 67 A6
Ammanford
= Rhydaman 22 E5
Amroth 20 F3
Anchor 41 B8
Anelog 50 C3
Anfield 72 A2
Angle 16 D3
Annscroft 49 B5
Anthony's Cross . 28 C4
Antrobus 73 D7
Apperley 29 B7
Appleton 72 B5
Appleton Park . . . 73 C7
Appleton Thorn . . 73 C7
Arberth
= Narberth 20 E2
Archenfield 36 D3
Arclid 65 B8
Arclid Green 65 B8
Arddleen 56 E2
Argoed 12 C3
Arle 29 C8
Arlebrook 29 F6
Arley 73 C8
Arley Green 73 C8
Arlingham 28 E4
Arno's Vale 6 B4
Arowry 57 A6
Arrowe Hill 71 B7

Arrow Green 37 A6
Arscott 48 B4
Arthog 52 F4
Ashbrook 49 E5
Ashchurch 29 A8
Ashcombe Park . . 5 D6
Ashford Bowdler 43 D8
Ashford
  Carbonell 43 D8
Ashgrove 7 E6
Ash Grove 63 F8
Ashleworth 29 B6
Ashley Down 6 A3
Ashley Moor 43 E7
Ash Magna 57 A8
Ashmead Green . 15 C7
Ash Parva 57 A8
Ashton Gate 6 B3
Ashton Heath . . . 73 D6
Ashton Vale 6 B3
Ashvale 25 E7
Asterley 48 B3
Asterton 48 E3
Astmoor 73 C5
Aston Crews 28 C3
Aston Cross 29 A8
Aston Ingham . . . 28 C3
Aston juxta
  Mondrum 65 C6
Aston Munslow . 43 A8
Aston on Carrant 29 A8
Aston on Clun . . 43 B5
Aston Pigott 48 B2
Aston Rogers . . . 48 B2
Aston Square . . . 56 C3
Atcham 49 B6
Auberrow 37 C7
Audlem 65 F6
Audley 65 D8
Aulden 37 B7
Aust 14 E3
Avening Green . . 15 D6
Avoncliff 7 E8
Avonmouth 6 A2
Awkley 14 E3
Awre 28 F4
Axbridge 5 F8
Axton 70 C4
Aylburton 14 B4
Aylburton
  Common 14 B4
Aylestone Hill . . . 37 D8
Aymestrey 43 E6

B

Babbinswood . . . 56 B3
Babel 34 E1
Babell 71 E5
Bachau 67 C5
Bache 43 B7
Bacheldre 47 E8
Bache Mill 43 A8
Bach-y-
  gwreiddyn 9 B7

Backe 21 D5
Backford 72 E3
Backford Cross . . 72 E2
Backwell 6 C1
Backwell
  Common 6 C1
Backwell Green . . 6 C1
Bacton 26 A5
Badgeworth 29 D8
Badminton 15 F8
Bae Cinmel
= Kinmel Bay 70 C1
Bae Colwyn
= Colwyn Bay . . . 69 D6
Bae Penrhyn
= Penrhyn Bay . . . 69 C6
Bagillt 71 D6
Bagley 57 C5
Bagley Marsh . . . 56 C4
Bagstone 15 E5
Bagwyllydiart . . . 27 B6
Bagwy Llydiart . . 27 B6
Bailbrook 7 C7
Baker's Hill 28 E1
Bala = Y Bala 54 A3
Baldwin's Gate . . 65 F8
Ballingham 28 A1
Ballingham Hill . . 28 A1
Balmer 57 B5
Balmer Heath . . . 57 B5
Balterley 65 D8
Balterley Green . . 65 D8
Balterley Heath . . 65 D7
Bamfurlong 29 C8
Bancffosfelen . . . 22 E2
Bancycapel 21 D8
Banc-y-Darren . . 39 B6
Bancyfelin 21 D6
Bancyffordd 31 E8
Bangor 67 E8
Bangor is y coed
= Bangor on Dee . . 63 E8
Bangor on Dee =
Bangor-is-y-coed . 63 E8
Bangor Teifi 31 D7
Bankshead 48 F2
Banwell 5 E7
Barbridge 65 C5
Bargoed 12 C2
Barkers Green . . . 57 C7
Barland 42 F3
Barmouth
= Abermaw 52 E4
Barnardtown 13 E6
Barnett Brook . . . 65 F5
Barnfields 37 D7
Barnwood 29 D7
Barons Cross . . . 37 A7
Barrack Hill 13 E6
Barrets Green . . . 64 C4
Barrow 29 C7
Barrow
  Common 6 C2
Barrow
  Gurney 6 C2

Barrow's Green . . 73 B5
Barrow Vale 6 D4
Barrow Wake . . . 29 D8
Barry Dock 4 C2
Barry Island 4 C2
Barthomley 65 D8
Bartington 73 D7
Barton End 15 C8
Barton Hill 6 B4
Bartonsham 37 E8
Baschurch 57 D5
Basford 43 A5
Bassaleg 12 E5
Batch 5 E6
Batchcott 43 D7
Bate Heath 73 D8
Bateman's Hill . . 17 D6
Bath 7 C7
Bathampton 7 C7
Batheaston 7 C7
Bathford 7 C7
Bathwick 7 C7
Battlefield 57 E7
Baysham 28 B1
Bayston Hill 49 B5
Beachley 14 D3
Beacon Hill 7 C7
Beambridge 49 F6
Bearwood 37 A5
Beaufort 25 E8
Beaumaris 68 D2
Beavan's Hill 28 C3
Bebington 72 C1
Beckjay 43 C5
Beddau 11 E8
Beddgelert 59 E7
Bedlinog 12 B1
Bedminster 6 B3
Bedminster Down . 6 C3
Bedstone 42 C5
Bedwas 12 E3
Bedwellty 12 B3
Bedwellty Pits . . 12 A3
Bedwlwyn 56 A1
Bed-y-coedwr . . 53 C6
Beechen Cliff 7 D7
Beechwood 73 C5
Began 12 F4
Begelly 17 C8
Beggar's Bush . . 42 F3
Beggars Pound . . 3 C7
Beguildy 42 C1
Beili-glas 26 E4
Belan 47 C8
Belgrano 69 D9
Belle Vale 72 B3
Bell o' th' Hill 64 E3
Belluton 6 D4
Bencombe 15 C7
Bengal 19 C7
Benhall 29 C8
Benllech 67 C7
Bentham 29 D8
Bentlass 17 D5
Bentlawnt 48 C2

Longden Common 48 C4
Longhope 28 D3
Longhouse 7 D6
Longlevens 29 C7
Long Meadowend 43 B6
Longney 29 E5
Longnor 49 C5
Longnor Park 49 C5
Long Oak 56 D4
Longridge 29 F7
Longridge End 29 C6
Longview 72 A3
Longville in the Dale 49 E6
Longwell Green 7 B5
Longwood 49 B8
Loppington 57 C6
Lostock Gralam 73 D8
Lostock Green 73 E8
Loveston 17 C7
Lowbands 29 A5
Lowcross Hill 64 D2
Lowe 57 B7
Lower Bearwood 37 A5
Lower Bebington 71 C8
Lower Berry Hill 28 E1
Lower Breinton 37 E7
Lower Brynamman 23 E7
Lower Bullingham 37 E8
Lower Bunbury 64 C4
Lower Burton 37 A6
Lower Cam 15 B6
Lower Canada 5 E7
Lower Carden 64 D2
Lower Chapel 35 E5
Lower Dinchope 43 B7
Lower Down 42 B4
Lower Failand 6 B2
Lower Frankton 56 B4
Lower Freystrop 17 B5
Lower Hamswell 7 B6
Lower Hardwick 37 A6
Lower Harpton 42 F3
Lower Hayton 43 B8
Lower Hazel 14 E4
Lower Hergest 36 A3
Lower Hopton 56 D4
Lower Hordley 56 C4
Lower Kilcott 15 E7
Lower Kinnerton 63 B7
Lower Kinsham 42 F5
Lower Knowle 6 B3
Lower Langford 5 D9
Lower Ledwyche 43 D8
Lower Lode 29 A7
Lower Lydbrook 28 D1
Lower Lye 43 E6
Lower Machen 12 E4
Lower Maes-coed 26 A4
Lower Meend 14 B3
Lower Morton 14 D4
Lower Mountain 63 C7
Lower Netchwood 49 E8
Lower New Inn 13 C6
Lower Ochrwyth 12 E4
Lower Penarth 4 C3
Lower Porthkerry 3 C8
Lower Rabber 36 B3
Lower Rea 29 D6
Lower Sketty 9 D7
Lower Soudley 28 F3
Lower Stone 15 D5
Lower Stretton 73 C7
Lower Swainswick 7 C7
Lower Threapwood 64 F1
Lower Todding 43 C6
Lower Tuffley 29 E6
Lower Walton 73 B7
Lower Weare 5 F8
Lower Welson 36 B3
Lower Weston 7 C6
Lower Whitley 73 D7
Lower Wick 15 C6
Lower Wych 64 F2
Lowlands 13 C5
Loxton 5 E7
Luckington 15 F8
Lucton 43 F6
Ludchurch 20 E2
Ludlow 43 D8
Lugg Green 43 F7
Lugwardine 37 D9
Lulham 37 D6
Lulsgate Bottom 6 C2
Luntley 37 A5
Lunts Heath 72 B5
Lushcott 49 D7
Luston 43 F7
Luxley 28 C3
Lydbury North 42 A5
Lyde Cross 37 D8
Lydham 48 E2
Lydney 14 B4
Lydstep 17 E7
Lye Cross 6 D1
Lye Hole 6 D2
Lymm 73 B8
Lympsham 5 F6
Lynchgate 42 A5
Lyneal 57 B5
Lyneal Mill 57 B6
Lyneal Wood 57 B6
Lyne Down 28 A2
Lyonshall 36 A4
Lypiatt 29 F8
Lythbank 49 B5

M

Machen 12 E4
Machroes 51 C6
Machynlleth 45 C5
Maddox Moor 17 B5
Madeley 65 F8
Madeley Heath 65 E8
Madeley Park 65 F8
Madley 37 E6
Maenaddwyn 67 C6
Maenclochog 20 B1
Maendy 3 A7
Maentwrog 60 F1
Maen-y-groes 31 A7
Maerdy 22 C5
Maes-bangor 39 B6
Maesbrook 56 D2
Maesbury 56 C3
Maesbury Marsh 56 C3
Maes-glas 13 E5
Maes Glas =Greenfield 71 D5
Maesgwyn-Isaf 47 A7
Maeshafn 62 B5
Maesllyn 31 D7
Maes llyn 31 D7
Maesmynis 35 C5
Maes Pennant 71 D5
Maes-Treylow 42 E3
Maesybont 22 D4
Maesycoed 11 E8
Maesycrugiau 32 D2
Maesycwmmer 12 D3
Maes-y-dre 63 B5
Maesygwartha 26 E2
Maesymeillion 31 C8
Maesypandy 46 D3
Maesyrhandir 47 E5
Magor 13 E8
Maiden Head 6 C3
Maiden Wells 17 E5
Main 55 E8
Maindee 13 E6
Maindy 4 A3
Mainstone 48 F1
Maisemore 29 C6
Malehurst 48 B3
Malkin's Bank 65 C8
Malltraeth 67 F5
Mallwyd 45 A8
Malswick 28 B4
Mamhilad 13 B6
Manafon 47 C6
Mancot 71 F8
Mancot Royal 71 F8
Mangotsfield 7 A5
Manian-fawr 30 C3
Manley Common 72 E5
Manmoel 12 B3
Manorbier 17 E7
Manorbier Newton 17 E6
Manordeilo 23 B6
Manorowen 19 B6
Mansel Lacy 37 C6
Mansell Gamage 37 D5
Marbury 64 E4
Marchamley 57 C8
Marchamley Wood 57 B8
Marchroes 51 C6
Marchwiel 63 E8
Marcross 3 C5
Marden 37 C8
Mardu 42 B3
Mardy 26 D4
Marford 63 C8
Margam 10 E2
Marian 70 D3
Marian Cwm 70 D3
Mariandyrys 68 C2
Marianglas 67 C7
Markham 12 B3
Marksbury 7 D5
Marlas 27 B6
Marlbrook 37 B8
Marley Green 64 E4
Marloes 16 C1
Marros 20 F4
Marshall's Cross 72 A5
Marshbrook 48 F4
Marsh Common 14 F3
Marshfield 12 F5
Marshfield Bank 65 C6
Marston 36 A5
Marston Stannett 37 A9
Marstow 28 D1
Martinscroft 73 B8
Martletwy 17 B6
Maryland 14 A2
Mascle Bridge 17 C5
Mathern 14 D2
Mathry 19 C5
Matson 29 D6
Maund Bryan 37 B9
Mawdlam 10 F3
Maw Green 65 C7
Mayals 9 D7
Mayeston 17 D6
Mayhill 9 D7
May Hill 27 E8
May Hill Village 28 C4
May's Green 5 D7
Mayshill 15 F5
Meadgate 7 E5
Meadowtown 48 C2
Mearns 7 E5
Medlicott 48 E4
Meer Common 36 B5
Meidrim 21 C5
Meifod 61 C8
Meinciau 22 E2
Meliden =Gallt Melyd 70 C3
Melinbyrhedyn 45 D7
Melin Caiach 12 C2
Melincourt 10 B3
Melin-y-coed 60 B4
Melin-y-ddôl 47 B5
Melin-y-grug 46 B5
Melin-y-Wig 62 E1
Melverley 56 E3
Melverley Green 56 E3
Menai Bridge =Porthaethwy 67 E8
Meole Brace 49 A5
Meols 71 A6
Merbach 36 C4
Merehead 57 A6
Mere Heath 73 E8
Merlin's Bridge 16 B4
Merlin's Cross 17 D5
Merrington 57 D6
Merrion 16 E4
Merthyr Cynog 34 E4
Merthyr-Dyfan 4 C2
Merthyr Mawr 2 A4
Merthyr Tydfil 25 F5
Merthyr Vale 11 C8
Methlem 50 B3
Michaelchurch 27 B8
Michaelchurch Escley 36 F4
Michaelchurch on Arrow 36 B2
Michaelston-le-Pit 4 B3
Michaelston-y-Fedw 12 F4
Michealston-super-Ely 4 A2
Mickle Trafford 72 F3
Middle Bridge 6 A1
Middle Hill 17 B5
Middlehope 49 F5
Middle Madeley 65 E8
Middle Maes-coed 36 F4
Middle Street 15 B7
Middleton Baggot 49 E8
Middleton on the Hill 43 F8
Middleton Priors 49 E8
Middle Wick 15 C6
Middleyard 15 B8
Midford 7 D7
Midsomer Norton 7 F5
Milbury Heath 15 D5
Milebrook 42 D4
Milford Haven 16 C4
Milkwall 28 F1
Millend 15 A7
Millhalf 36 C3
Millin Cross 17 B5
Milner's Heath 64 B2
Milo 22 D4
Milton End 28 E4
Milwr 71 E5
Minera 63 D6
Minffordd 45 A5
Minllyn 54 F2
Minshull Vernon 65 B6
Minsterley 48 C3
Minsterworth 29 D5
Minton 48 E4
Minwear 17 B6
Miserden 29 F8
Miskin 11 F7
Mitcheldean 28 D3
Mitchel Troy 27 E7
Mitcheltroy Common 27 F7
Moblake 65 F6
Moccas 36 D5
Mochdre 69 D6
Moelfre 67 B7
Moel Tryfan 59 C6
Moel-y-crio 71 F5
Moity 35 D8
Mold 63 B5
Monachty 38 F3
Monaughty 42 E2
Mondaytown 48 B2
Monington 30 D2
Monkhopton 49 E8
Monkland 37 A7
Monknash 3 B5
Monkton Combe 7 D7
Monkton Farleigh 7 C8
Monmarsh 37 C8
Monmouth =Trefynwy 27 E8
Monmouth Cap 27 B5
Monnington on Wye 36 D5
Montford Bridge 57 E5
Montgomery 47 D8
Montpelier 6 B3
Moorcot 36 A5
Moore 73 C6
Moorhampton 37 C5
Moorledge 6 D3
Môrawelon 66 C2
Morda 56 C2
More 48 E2
Moreton Corbet 57 D8
Moreton on Lugg 37 C8
Moreton Valence 29 F5
Morfa Bach 21 E7
Morfa Bychan 52 A2
Morfa Dinlle 58 C4
Morfa Glas 24 F2
Morfa Nefyn 58 F1
Morfydd 62 E3
Morganstown 12 F2
Moriah 38 C5
Mork 14 A3
Morristown 4 B3
Mortimer's Cross 43 F6
Morton Common 56 D2
Morton Mill 57 D8
Moss Bank 73 B5
Mossbrow 73 B9
Mossley Hill 72 B2
Moston 65 B7
Moston Green 65 B7
Mostyn 71 C5
Mostyn Quay 71 C5
Mouldsworth 72 E5
Mountain 66 C1
Mountain Air 25 F8
Mountain Ash =Aberpennar 11 C7
Mountain Water 19 E6
Mount Ballan 14 E1
Mount Hill 7 B5
Mounton 14 D2
Mount Sion 63 D6
Moylgrove =Trewyddel 30 D2
Much Birch 27 A8
Much Dewchurch 27 A7
Much Marcle 28 A3
Much Wenlock 49 C8
Munslow 49 F6
Munstone 37 D8
Murch 4 B3
Murdishaw 73 C6
Murrell's End 28 A4
Musselwick 16 C2
Mwdwl-eithin 71 D5
Mwynbwll 71 F5
Myddfai 23 B8
Myddle 57 D6
Myddlewood 57 D6
Myddyn-fych 23 E5
Mydroilyn 32 A2
Mynachdy 4 A3
Mynachlog-ddu 20 A2
Mynd 42 D5
Myndd Llandegai 59 A8
Myndtown 48 F3
Mynydd Bach 39 C7
Mynydd-bach 14 D1
Mynydd Bodafon 67 B6
Mynydd Fflint =Flint Mountain 71 E6
Mynydd Gilan 51 D5
Mynydd-isa 63 B6
Mynyddislwyn 12 D3
Mynydd-llan 71 E5
Mynydd Marian 69 D7
Mynydd Mechell 66 B4
Mynyddygarreg 21 F8
Mynytho 51 B6
Myrtle Hill 23 A8
Mytton 57 E5

N

Naid-y-march 71 D5
Nailbridge 28 D2
Nailsea 6 B1
Nailwell 7 D6
Nanhoron 51 B5
Nanhyfer =Nevern 30 E1
Nannau 53 D6
Nannerch 71 F5
Nant 21 D8
Nant Alyn 62 A4
Nant-ddu 25 D5
Nanternis 31 A7
Nantgaredig 22 C2
Nantgarw 12 E2
Nant-glas 40 F4
Nantglyn 61 B8
Nantgwyn 40 C4
Nantlle 59 D6
Nantmawr 56 D2
Nant Mawr 63 B6
Nantmel 41 E5
Nantmor 59 E8
Nant Peris =Old Llanberis 59 C8
Nantserth 40 D4
Nant Uchaf 61 C8
Nantwich 65 D6
Nant-y-Bai 33 D8
Nant-y-Bwch 25 E7
Nant-y-cafn 24 F1
Nantycaws 22 D2
Nant y Caws 56 C2
Nant-y-ceisiad 12 E4
Nant-y-derry 13 A6
Nant-y-felin 68 E3
Nant-y-ffin 22 A4
Nantyglo 26 E1
Nant-y-gollen 56 C1
Nant-y-moel 11 D5
Nant-y-pandy 68 E3
Nant-y-Rhiw 60 C4
Nantyronen Station 39 C6
Narberth =Arberth 20 E2
Narberth Bridge 20 E2
Nasareth 58 D5
Nastend 15 A7
Natton 29 A8
Nebo 67 A6
Neenton 49 F8
Nefod 56 A3
Nefyn 58 F2
Neinthirion 46 B3
Nelly Andrews Green 48 B1
Nelson 12 C2
Nempnett Thrubwell 6 D2
Nercwys 63 B5
Nesscliffe 56 E4
Nessholt 71 D8
Neston 71 D7
Netham 6 B4
Netherend 14 B3
Nether Skyborry 42 D3
Nettleton 29 E8
Nettleton Green 7 A8
Nettleton Shrub 7 A8